The Unauthorized Jesus

Investigating the Hidden Teachings
and Dark Side of the Biblical Christ

Richard L Haight

Shinkaikan Body, Mind, Spirit LLC
www.richardlhaight.com

Disclaimer: This book is a critical analysis of a set of ideas and textual patterns found within the Bible and their historical consequences. It is not intended as a critique of any group of people, be they Christian, Jewish, or Muslim. The patterns described in this book are universal human tendencies, and the goal of this work is to understand, not to condemn.

ISBN: 978-1-956889-24-6

Published by Shinkaikan Body, Mind, Spirit LLC
Rogue River, Oregon
www.richardlhaight.com

Table of Contents

Introduction

Welcome to the first forensic investigation of the New Testament in two thousand years.

You might think that in all this time, with billions of readers, someone would have already done what this book does. But to my utter astonishment, it seems no one has. By the time you finish reading, you may wonder how it is possible that the most scrutinized book in human history has never been diagnosed in this way.

I did not start this project intending to deconstruct Jesus. That was never my goal. My motivation was to clarify the true teachings of Christ, driven by a recurring dream that has haunted me since childhood.

I was eight years old when the dreams began, dreams that felt more real than waking life. In them, Jesus of Nazareth lay on the floor before me—boneless. His body was soft, collapsing into itself like a sack of flesh. His eyes were gentle, yet filled with a sorrow deeper than anything I had ever seen.

He spoke to me:

> *Find my bones. They are the core of my teaching.*
> *Most of what is written about me is untrue.*
> *Mankind has twisted my message for selfish gain,*
> *until almost nothing of its essence remains.*

This book is the fulfillment of that promise. It reads like a fast-paced, reluctant detective story, but it does so by treating the vast richness of two millennia of theological tradition as a body of evidence rather than as a theological debate.

That approach unravels everything. This investigation is a search for those "bones": the authentic teaching buried beneath layers of doctrine, history, and misdirection.

This book will almost certainly not suit you if you are satisfied with the teachings of Christianity as you know them. If you hold unshakeable ideas about who Jesus is, his mission, and his teachings, this investigation will challenge you in ways you may not welcome. This is an unflinching attempt to distinguish authentic teachings from what may have obscured them.

But if you are willing to set aside your conclusions, if only for the duration of this reading, and look at the evidence with fresh eyes, then you are ready for this investigation. It is an exercise in radical integrity: taking a character at his word and measuring his actions against that standard, without exception.

Our investigation operates under a single, demanding principle: to take the character of Jesus as he is written and hold him to his own stated standards, following the evidence wherever it leads. To do this, we will read the Bible as its most fervent believers demand, as a literal, cohesive account, but with one critical adjustment: we will grant no special exemptions frameworks that veil the text.

Why? If Jesus is God, he will be the perfect example of all his teachings.

Therefore, where this literal reading exposes a contradiction or a theological conundrum, we will not attempt to explain it away. No "historical accidents," no "divine mysteries." Instead, we will ask a more direct question: What happens when we hold this text to the very standard its defenders claim it meets?

If Jesus taught "judge not," we will notice every time he judged.
If he taught "let your yes be yes," we will track when his no became yes.
If he taught "forgive absolutely," we will see whom he condemned.

Some may find this process ruthless. Why highlight every contradiction? Think of it as a winnowing process. To find the edible grain, the wheat must be thrashed and thrown against the wind so the chaff can be blown away. If we are gentle with the chaff, we don't get to the edible wheat. We are not attacking the truth; we are aggressively removing everything that veils it. We are breaking the shell to find the pearl. We will use the art of the question as our thrashing instrument.

This path of questioning began for me as a child, just before the dreams. My Bible study teacher told me my parents would burn in Hell unless they became born-again Christians. When I rushed home, terrified, to convert them, my father met my fear with gentle questions that would define my life:

"Is it loving to send someone to Hell for eternity just because they weren't born-again Christians? If you were God, would you send us to Hell for not being the right kind of Christian?"

That honest questioning is the spirit of this book. We are not here to attack or defend, but to see. We are here to honor the questioning child in each of us who simply wants the story to make sense. This investigation is about seeing what is written on the page, not what we have been told is there.

If you are committed to following evidence regardless of where it leads, you are ready for this investigation. If not, I understand.

Jesus had been my hero since childhood. When other kids imagined they were Superman or Batman, I imagined I was Jesus—saving people through miracles and wise teachings. Even after I left Christianity, that love never faded.

These revelations cost me the comfort of my lifelong hero. They may cost you something too. But maybe that cost is the price of seeing clearly.

Once we have reached that clarity, having successfully separated the wheat from the chaff, we will expand out to see how these ancient divisive patterns are still active today, shaping policy and belief for billions of people and pushing nuclear-armed nations closer to war than at any point in human history.

It's time to open our eyes.

What if for two thousand years, we've been reading the story, but not seeing it? Hearing the words, but not hearing the voice beneath them?

The dreams kept returning—"Find my bones." This book is that investigation. Won't you join me in seeing it through?

Rules of the Investigation

Before our detective work begins, it is crucial to lay out the rules that govern this book. This is a specific exercise in textual analysis that has never been done with the Bible. We are setting a precedent, and we must get it right. To ensure a fair and transparent investigation, let's proceed from a shared understanding of the terms.

1. The Biblical Jesus is Our Only Subject.
The name "Jesus" can refer to many concepts: the historical man, the theological figure, the "ascended master" of New Age spirituality, or the Jesus of personal mystical experience. Our investigation is not concerned with these other figures. Our scene of the investigation is the Bible itself, and our discipline as detectives requires us to look *only* at the evidence found within its pages. Our task is to analyze the character as he is written, taking him at his word.

2. We Will Read the Text as a Unified Narrative.
For two thousand years, there have been two primary ways of approaching biblical contradictions. The metaphorical approach views the text as a collection of allegories, where inconsistencies are not as important as the spiritual lessons. For a long time, this was my own view.

But I came to realize that if a text is read purely as metaphor, it can be made to mean almost anything. It becomes a mirror for our own beliefs, not a body of evidence to be examined. The patterns, the hypocrisies, the fingerprints: everything we are here to investigate can be missed entirely.

The literalist approach, on the other hand, insists the Bible is a cohesive, inerrant account of history. We will accept the literalist claim at face value and read the four Gospels as a single, coherent story—exactly the way its most fervent believers say it should be read.

4

The only adjustment we will make is this: whenever something feels inconsistent or contradictory, we will investigate and document it. We will not explain it away, harmonize it, or use metaphor to explain it. We will let the text speak for itself and follow the evidence wherever it leads.

If the story truly holds together as literalists insist, it will stand beautifully on its own. If it does not, the cracks will appear naturally, and we will winnow away that chaff together.

Once our detective work is complete, we can always return to a metaphorical view if we wish.

3. Jesus's Own Standard is the Only Measure.
"By their fruits you will know them." This is the standard Jesus himself provides. In this investigation, he will be held to his own measure, with no special exemptions or theological escape hatches. Applying this principle requires discipline. It was the hardest part of the process for me. Our natural impulse is to grant the "benefit of the doubt" to figures we revere. I spent the first half of this investigation trying to save the Jesus I loved from the evidence I was finding. This book asks you to set that impulse aside and participate in an exercise in radical integrity, which means we must first document *what* the evidence shows before we speculate on *why*.

How "Author's Notes" Create Transparency
To maintain this integrity, I will sometimes step out of the main narrative to speak directly to you in sections marked as **"Author's Note"**. This system is part of our contract of fairness, and these notes serve four specific purposes:

1. To Provide Essential Context: To explain historical practices (Roman, Jewish) or define key Greek and Hebrew terms that are essential for understanding the narrative.

2. To Address Textual Problems: To point out, as a matter of intellectual fairness, significant issues within the text itself, such as:

- **Textual Variants:** Noting when a major story is absent from the oldest manuscripts.
- **Incoherence:** Acknowledging profound contradictions between Gospel accounts.

- o **Missing Stories:** Highlighting when a sensational event in one Gospel is ignored by the others.
- o **Accepting a Claim as Its Own Proof:** Treating a character's self-justification as objective fact without verifying it (e.g., "Jesus said he fulfilled the prophecy, so we don't need to check if the prophecy was actually about him").

3. To Maintain the Rules: To occasionally remind you of the specific rules of this investigation, especially when the mind is tempted to revert to old habits of reading.

These habits are often reflexive and can include:

- o **Explaining away** a difficult passage by assigning an unstated motive (e.g., "He did that to fulfill prophecy").
- o **Harmonizing** two conflicting accounts into a single story that isn't in the text.
- o Offering a **theological escape hatch** for a direct contradiction (e.g., "Jesus is God, so the rules don't apply to him").

4. To Identify Personal Speculation: To clearly label any moments where I offer a personal interpretation or an educated guess, ensuring a clear line between what the evidence says and where my own reasoning begins.

My goal in using this system is to empower you. It allows you to see the evidence, understand the textual problems, and distinguish my analysis from the source material. This transparency is what makes it possible to trust the process and, ultimately, to draw your own informed conclusions.

Part I

The Gospels

Our investigation begins here, with the foundational texts of Christianity: the four Gospels. For any reader who may be unfamiliar with the Bible's structure, it's helpful to understand where these books fit.

The Christian Bible is divided into two major sections. The Old Testament tells the story *leading up to* the time of Jesus—the history, laws, and prophecies of the Jewish people. The New Testament focuses on the life of Jesus and the community that formed after his death.

But even the New Testament has two distinct parts. It begins with the four Gospels—Matthew, Mark, Luke, and John. These are the primary biographical accounts of Jesus's birth, his teachings, his miracles, his ministry, and his death. The rest of the New Testament—books like Acts, the letters of Paul, and Revelation—is largely the story of the *aftermath*, detailing the growth of the early church and the theology that developed around the figure of Jesus.

For our investigation, these four Gospels are the primary evidence. They are the "scene of the investigation." This is the official narrative of Jesus's life as the tradition has preserved it.

Therefore, as we step into this first and most crucial part of our journey, I must ask you to join me in a specific discipline. Many of us come to these stories with years of interpretation already in our minds—from pastors, scholars, other books, or even just cultural osmosis. For Part I, our task is to set all of that aside.

Let's commit to reading this story as if for the first time, allowing the character of Jesus to reveal himself only through his own words and actions as recorded in these texts. We will measure the story only by the standards it sets for itself.

Chapter 1

The Test

I opened my Bible to trace Jesus's journey, expecting to find the perfect man from my childhood dreams. What I discovered in those first pages would begin to unravel everything I thought I knew.

Before the sermons, before the healings, before the crowds began to gather, there was the baptism followed by a test.

Jesus comes to the Jordan River. He finds John the Baptist, already gathering a crowd. John is calling people to repentance.

I thought about baptism and what it meant to them—this full-body immersion, washing away the past through symbolic drowning, while surrendering the personal self to God.

John's teaching was quite radical. His life and teachings resembled those of Isaiah. He lived in the wilderness, surviving on honey and locusts. He wasn't calling people to obey rituals, like other preachers. He was calling them to total transformation. He heralded the coming messiah and required complete dedication to God.

Matthew tells us that "people from Jerusalem, all of Judea, and all the region around the Jordan went out to him" (Mt 3:5). This was the most recognized prophet of the age, the one many believed was Elijah returned.

When Jesus requests baptism, John resists, saying, "I need to be baptized by you, and you come to me?" Jesus answers: "Allow it now, for this is the fitting way for us to fulfill all righteousness" (Mt 3:14–15).

So John agrees. Jesus steps into the water. He is submerged, then rises. And something extraordinary happens.

The Test

The heavens open. The Spirit descends like a dove. And a voice speaks: "This is my beloved Son, with whom I am well pleased" (Mt 3:17).

The crowd witnesses this divine endorsement. John sees it. The moment is public and unmistakable.

I could see that baptism was where Jesus's test began. This moment of radiant clarity, of unity, of God speaking and directing Jesus to *the test.*

Then, for forty days and nights, Jesus fasts alone in the wilderness.

Forty days. I tried to imagine it. I've fasted twice in the warmth of my own home for 15 days each. I had no energy and it was a struggle just to keep warm.

Jesus did it in the Judean desert—scorching by day, near-freezing at night. No food. The body consuming itself. It was a challenge far beyond what I experienced.

His mind must have been wavering between clarity and hallucination. By the end, he would have been skeletal, barely able to stand.

At the end of this trial, when he is weakest, *he is tempted by Satan.*

It is one of the most important scenes in the entire Gospel.

I say that because in this moment, we see Jesus face the same adversary that deceived Adam and Eve, the same that tormented Job, the same that whispers through every human mind.

But unlike Adam and Eve, Jesus did not bite.

Yet—

Here, at the very threshold of his ministry, Jesus demonstrated the principle by which we can track his entire path: incorruptible integrity. This was the key.

Even in weakness, even in hunger, even unto death, Jesus would not prioritize himself over God.

The Gospel of Matthew describes it like this: "Then Jesus was led up by the Spirit into the wilderness to be tempted by the devil. After fasting forty days and forty nights, he was hungry" (Mt 4:1–2).

Then comes the first temptation: "If you are the Son of God, command that these stones become bread" (Mt 4:3).

And Jesus replies: "It is written, 'Man shall not live by bread alone, but by every word that proceeds from the mouth of God'" (Mt 4:4).

He will not betray God, even for survival.

Next, he is transported to the temple pinnacle where the second temptation was offered: "If you are the Son of God, throw yourself down. For it is written: 'He will command his angels concerning you, and they will lift you up in their hands, so that you will not strike your foot against a stone'" (Mt 4:6).

Notice that Satan quotes scripture to Jesus—using God's own words as a weapon.

Jesus maintains integrity saying, "Again, it is written, 'You shall not test the Lord, your God'" (Mt 4:7).

Finally comes the third temptation: "The devil took him to a very high mountain and showed him all the kingdoms of the world and their splendor. 'All this I will give you,' he said, 'if you will bow down and worship me'" (Mt 4:8-9).

And Jesus says: "Get behind me, Satan! For it is written, 'You shall worship the Lord your God, and you shall serve him only'" (Mt 4:10).

Jesus maintained his integrity under extreme pressures that would cause almost any other human to fail.

I understood that these responses in the desert, combined with what he teaches through what we call the Sermon on the Mount, became the foundation of wisdom he'd later teach:

- o Do not use the power of God even to save your own life.
- o Do not test God.
- o Do not glorify yourself.
- o Do not judge.
- o Love your enemies.
- o Forgive absolutely.
- o You reap what you sow.

These values and teachings provide the means by which we can examine Jesus fairly and respectfully.

When Jesus passes this test, Satan departs. Angels come. The test was over. Or so it seemed.

But as I continued reading, I noticed something curious. Satan had vanished from the narrative, but his voice—that same voice that offered glory, that quoted scripture for its own purposes, that promised kingdoms—seemed to echo in unexpected places.

I remembered the story of Job, how Satan had appeared in God's court not as a rebel, but as an examiner.

"And God said, 'Have you considered my servant Job?'" Satan responds: "Does Job fear God for nothing?" *Take away the success and comfort,* Satan argues, "and he will renounce you to your face" (Job 1:8-11).

In the story of Job, God allows the test. In the story of Jesus, God initiates it.

Satan, true to his nature, does not waste his best attacks. He waits. He watches.

So, as we continue the story, remember: Satan has not left the stage.

He has simply gone quiet, waiting for his moment.

Chapter 2

The Voices

It was the afternoon of Good Friday, and I wasn't even thinking about Jesus when it happened. I was working on a fictional story, jotting down notes about the characters, when an insight struck with sudden clarity.

Jesus speaks in three distinct voices!

The insight stunned me for a moment. Christianity teaches that he speaks in two voices, the voice of God and the voice of man. We have been taught to read him through those two voices.

But, it seems, there is another voice. In that moment, I could feel the nature of each voice as clearly as if they were speaking in the room. I knew—*knew* with my whole body—that if I read scripture listening for these voices, I would find what Jesus asked of me—*the bones of Christ.*

Specific quotations, one after another, flashed into my head. I quickly wrote them down, not wanting to lose them.

In retrospect, I can see that those specific quotations had etched themselves in my mind during childhood. The realization of the three voices dislodged them, so they could float to the surface of my mind.

After jotting them down, I checked my Bible to compare my memory of scripture to the source material for accuracy. Though my quotations were not exact, the essential point was spot on. Jesus did appear to speak in three distinct voices.

One of the first examples that came to mind was from the story of the rich man. When the man addressed him as "Good Teacher," Jesus's response always struck me. He didn't accept the praise. Instead, he corrected the man: "Why do you call me good? No one is good, except one—God" (Mk 10:18).

To me, this was an honest man making a distinction. A human voice, not taking unfair credit.

I flipped pages, hunting for the next quote. I've always had a poor memory for verses. I can't always remember who said what or what the verse numbers are. So, I checked Bible Gateway, an online site that has a search function.

I entered in a few key words from my quote, and the original text came up: "But I tell you, love your enemies, bless those who curse you, do good to those who hate you, and pray for those who mistreat you and persecute you" (Mt 5:44).

Yes. There it was. The voice of unconditional love. Pure. Clear. Divine. This was a unifying voice. Not all passages conveyed that same unifying message, though.

Then my eyes caught Luke 14:26, a verse I've always felt strong aversion to: "If anyone comes to me, and doesn't disregard his own father, mother, wife, children, brothers, and sisters, yes, and his own life also, he can't be my disciple."

Divisiveness—was this a divine voice? Disregard those who depend upon you? It seems completely incompatible with the teachings of unconditional love and service Jesus is known for.

"Disregard" didn't match my memory of this passage from other translations, so I checked the original Greek. There the word is *miseō*, which means "hate." The NIV and NRSV use that stronger rendering, while the World English Bible softens it in the main text to "disregard," with a footnote noting "or, hate."

Hate your family to follow Jesus? That's even more disturbing than "disregard."

This stark difference convinced me I was onto something important. If Jesus really spoke in multiple voices, then tracking these variations—and checking the original Greek when needed—would be crucial to understanding his complete message.

Author's Note: *I use the World English Bible (WEB) throughout this analysis, as its public domain status allows for the extensive quotation necessary for* *detailed textual examination. When translation choices significantly alter meaning, as with "disregard" versus "hate" in this passage, I'll note the original Greek and compare major translations to ensure accuracy.*

The more I read that night, the clearer the voices became. Sometimes Jesus spoke as a human soul seeking God. Sometimes divine clarity poured through him. And sometimes—he spoke from a darker voice.

As I started hunting for these voices in scripture, that word—*sin*—kept appearing. But *sin* in Greek (*hamartia*) doesn't mean wickedness, as we tend to think of it. It means to miss the mark. Like an archer whose arrow flies wide.

Suddenly I could see how this "missing the mark" idea helped me distinguish between the voices. Let's explore some more examples of the three voices to dial them in.

Jesus the human being said this when he felt dread about his mission to be crucified: "Father, if you are willing, remove this cup from me. Nevertheless, not my will, but yours, be done." (Lk 22:42). It represents doubt, insecurity, fear, but with a final determination to follow through according to God's will.

The holy voice said this: "Therefore, whatever you desire for men to do to you, you shall also do to them; for this is the law and the prophets" (Mt 7:12). It's a healing, forgiving, unifying voice.

The dark voice, by contrast, sows the seeds of separation and twists legitimate needs into self-service. When a gentile woman (non-Jew) asked Jesus for help he replied: "It is not appropriate to take the children's bread and throw it to the dogs." (Mt 15:24-26). It's a cruel and judgmental voice.

As I traced this voice throughout the night, a general pattern emerged—it whispers, "*Make it about you.*"

Isn't that the voice of Ego?

To be clear, when I use this term, I am not referring to a modern psychological concept. I am pointing directly to a pattern of consciousness described within the Bible itself: the **self-exalting** ambition of "Lucifer" in Isaiah who declared, "I will make myself like the Most High!"; the **glory-seeking** of Satan in the desert who demanded, "bow down and worship me"; and his **accusatory judgments** that divide us into good and evil, worthy and unworthy. This voice is full of hypocrisy and self-aggrandizement. This, for our investigation, is the voice of Ego.

With that definition established, what then is its opposite? If the dark voice is Ego, the divine voice must be Love. My investigation assumes that the primary aim, the ultimate integrity, is alignment with a loving, unifying God.

This standard is set by Jesus himself. When a scribe asked him what the most important commandment was, Jesus was unequivocal. He quoted two commands that, for him, formed the bedrock of everything:

First: "You shall love the Lord your God with all your heart, and with all your soul, and with all your mind, and with all your strength."

And second: "You shall love your neighbor as yourself."

Jesus concludes, "There is no other commandment greater than these" (Mk 12:30-31).

But later Jesus takes this commandment to its absolute limit, defining the divine voice with a teaching that stands in perfect opposition to the Ego. In the Sermon on the Mount, he says:

"You have heard that it was said, 'You shall love your neighbor and hate your enemy.' But I tell you, **love your enemies,** bless those who curse you, do good to those who hate you, and pray for those who mistreat you and persecute you" (Mt 5:43-44).

This is the ultimate standard. Not just loving your neighbor, but loving your enemy. This unconditional, boundary-dissolving love, often called *agape*, aims for the good of all without exception. It is the very essence of a unifying God.

This, then, gives us the two opposing forces that will be at the heart of our investigation. On one side, we have the dark voice of **Ego**: the self-exalting, glory-seeking pattern that divides the world through condemnatory judgments. On the other, we have the divine voice of **Love (*Agape*)**: the unifying, selfless drive to love all, even one's enemies, without condition.

Is that fair?

As I traced the voices through that long night, marking passages, the pattern became undeniable.

The human voice appeared in moments of genuine vulnerability and fear. The voice of harmony rang out with unmistakable clarity and love. But that third voice—I found it in places that had always made me uncomfortable:

- He cursed a fig tree for not bearing fruit out of season (Mk 11:14; Mt 21:19).
- He called a Canaanite woman a dog (Mt 15:26).
- He said: "Don't think that I came to send peace on the earth. I didn't come to send peace, but a sword. For I came to set a man at odds against his father, and a daughter against her mother, and a daughter-in-law against her mother-in-law. A man's foes will be those of his own household" (Mt 10:34-36).

It seemed to me that the voices revealed something we might have missed. And I could see that even Jesus, who was called "the Son of God," carried the whisper of the adversary—Ego.

I had been up almost all night researching and writing. For the next two days, I wrote in a fever state, barely sleeping, driven by a mysterious clarity that felt directed. By Easter evening, the barebones rough draft was done.

Finally, I sat in the silence of recognition. The unfounded belief I'd carried about Jesus since childhood, that every word was pure divine wisdom, had been shattered. But in its place, something more profound was emerging.

If Jesus carried all three voices, just like us—if he faced the same inner war we all face, then maybe his story wasn't about worshipping perfection from afar.

We could look at the story of Jesus as a map, with the key to this map being the three voices. And once you hear them, really hear them, you can never read these texts the same way again. Let's see where those voices lead us.

Author's Note: *Before we begin our exploration, it's crucial to remember the specific rules of our investigation. A historian might attribute conflicting voices to different authors or scribal editing. A theologian might try to harmonize them. We are doing neither. We are taking the final text as a single character profile— and listening for the inconsistencies within that one character. A simple marker for these voices is the degree of integrity that they represent.* **Be a master detective, overlooking nothing.**

Chapter 3

Early Miracles, Shifting Voices

After the desert, Jesus steps into the public eye. He speaks. He heals. He performs miracles. And he gathers followers. To the world, this is the moment his greatness begins.

But before we dive deeper into his miraculous acts, I need to address something that's probably on your mind.

Did these miracles actually happen? Water into wine? Healing the blind? Raising the dead?

I wrestled with this question for years. Here's what I understood: for the purposes of our exploration, which is to see the meaning in the narrative, it's best to imagine that Jesus is real, and that God and miracles, Satan and sin are real.

If we listen closely, not just to what he says or does, but for the *source* of his miracles, his actions, and his teachings, we begin to sense an important truth: Not all of his words and actions come from the same place. And that thought brings my mind to the miracle at Cana.

John 2:1–11 tells the story: At a wedding in Cana, when the wine runs out, Jesus's mother asks him to help. Jesus responds, "Woman, what does that have to do with you and me? My hour has not yet come." But when his mother tells the servants to do whatever Jesus says, he proceeds to turn water into wine anyway. John notes this "revealed his glory; and his disciples believed in him."

I read this passage multiple times before the contradiction hit me. Jesus says no. My hour has not yet come. *Then he does it anyway.*

Wait. In the desert, what had Jesus refused to do? He would not compromise integrity for any reason, but at Cana, he uses divine power to solve ... a social embarrassment?

Wasn't this the weakness of a human Jesus seeking to please his mother? Maybe. But as I read closer, another voice emerged.

He performs a miracle in public, creating spectacle. The writer of John explicitly tells us why: "through which he revealed his glory. "

Glory? Hadn't Satan just offered Jesus all the glory of the kingdoms? And hadn't Jesus refused? So why was John celebrating Jesus revealing his glory?

I stared at the page, my mind reeling.

He wouldn't use divine power even to save his own life in the desert. But here, he uses that same power to make wine for a party?

And his mother. Notice how this unfolds. She makes the request. He says no. She ignores his refusal and tells the servants to obey him anyway.

Was his weakness family pressure? The desire to be a good son? The pull to be seen as special?

"Woman, what does that have to do with you and me? My hour has not yet come." He knows it's not time. He knows it's not right. *But he does it anyway.*

The same man who wouldn't compromise principle to save his own life had just compromised? Was *this* the voice of integrity that wouldn't have acted against its own stated timing?

The standard explanation says that Jesus was honoring his parents as Jewish tradition required. But this is the same Jesus who broke traditions and defied family whenever God's will demanded it. He'd just declared "My hour has not yet come"—yet he acted anyway.

What happened to "Let your 'Yes' be 'Yes' and your 'No' be 'No.' Whatever is more than these is of the evil one" (Mt 5:37)?"

But at Cana, his no wasn't no. He said his hour had not yet come—then acted anyway. Which voice was speaking? This wasn't what I was expecting to find from Jesus. But maybe I was reading too much into it? Maybe there was an explanation I was missing?

Maybe that was the voice of Ego, seeking glory. What of the divine voice?

I needed a clear, undeniable example of the divine voice, a moment where the clouds of ego and human frailty parted, revealing something clean and whole.

I wasn't looking for a spectacle of power—not a mountain moved or a sea parted. I was listening for a different kind of miracle: a miracle of wisdom, of compassion that cuts through the noise of judgment, that had nothing to do with self-glorification.

And then I remembered the story that most inspired me as a child. It's a story set not in a quiet Galilean town, but in the heart of the conflict: the temple in Jerusalem. The tension is high. The authorities are actively trying to trap Jesus.

John 8:2-11 tells the story:

Early in the morning, he came again into the temple, and all the people came to him. He sat down and taught them. The scribes and the Pharisees brought a woman taken in adultery. Having set her in the middle, they told him, "Teacher, this woman has been caught in the act of adultery. Now in our law, Moses commanded us to stone such women. What then do you say?" They said this testing him, that they might have something to accuse him of.

But Jesus stooped down and wrote on the ground with his finger. But when they continued asking him, he lifted himself up and said to them, "He who is without sin among you, let him throw the first stone at her." Again he stooped down and wrote on the ground.

They, when they heard it, being convicted by their conscience, went out one by one, beginning from the oldest to the last. Jesus was left alone with the woman standing in the middle. Jesus, standing up, saw her and said, "Woman, where are your accusers? Did no one condemn you?"

She said, "No one, Lord."

Jesus said, "Neither do I condemn you. Go your way. From now on, sin no more."

I read the passage again and again. Here, there was no quest for glory. No self-aggrandizing pronouncement. Just a quiet, masterful dismantling of hypocrisy.

The strategy was masterful. He does not engage their argument on their terms. He refuses to participate in their judgment. Instead, he turns the very act of judgment back upon the accusers, forcing them into a moment of self-reflection. He doesn't condemn them; he simply holds up a mirror, and they recognize their hearts and walk away.

And then, in the quiet aftermath, he turns to the woman, and says, "Neither do I condemn you." It is a moment of pure, unearned grace. This is the voice that blesses the merciful and comforts those who mourn. It is the voice that commands us to "Judge not."

This was my childhood hero.

This was the Jesus I hoped to find.

Chapter 4

The Escalation

The Pharisees came to Jesus in public and demanded a miracle. According to Jesus, they did this to trap him, because they didn't believe. They wanted to bait him into a crowded performance, then call it fraud, destroying his reputation publicly.

Then some of the scribes and Pharisees answered, 'Teacher, we want to see a sign from you.' But he answered them, 'An evil and adulterous generation seeks after a sign, but no sign will be given to it but the sign of Jonah the prophet. For as Jonah was three days and three nights in the belly of the huge fish, so will the Son of Man be three days and three nights in the heart of the earth'" (Mt 12:38–40).

I read those words and felt something twist in my stomach.

On the surface, this looked like spiritual strength. Jesus refuses to perform on demand. He won't turn his power into a circus act. He offers something cryptic instead, a reference to his coming death and resurrection.

But "An evil and adulterous generation" (Mt 12:39 and Mt 16:4): Isn't he judging them? Publicly. Harshly.

This public condemnation feels like the polar opposite of the godly man who commanded, "Love your enemies, bless those who curse you, do good to those who hate you, and pray for those who mistreat you" (Mt 5:44). It feels like he's delivering the slap, rather than turning the other cheek.

What happened to the divine voice that taught in Luke 6:37, "Don't judge, and you won't be judged. Don't condemn, and you won't be condemned. Set free, and you will be set free"?

I looked up these passages again, trying to reconcile what I was seeing.

Wasn't his judgment sin? Wasn't Jesus missing the mark of his own stated principles? In disbelief, I reread the passage: "Evil and adulterous"—wasn't that venom in his words?

But then I thought, these were the Pharisees. Weren't they the bad guys? Weren't they corrupt hypocrites who deserved what they got?

The bad guys? Where did I get that impression? From my Bible Study teacher as a child. And where did she get it from? Jesus?

Weren't we all sinning for Jesus? I was beginning to feel hypocritical. I'd been judging the Pharisees for most of my life.

I forced myself to slow down. I had been judging, and that's not right. I had never given the Pharisees a fair shake. I began to really consider their position.

Who exactly were these groups Jesus was attacking? I searched the New Testament for a clear definition of the Pharisees and the Sadducees to see if Jesus's animosity made sense.

What I found in the Book of Acts revealed a puzzling contradiction.

In Acts 23:6–8, the Apostle Paul stands trial. To save himself, he exploits a fundamental divide between the two groups. The text explicitly states the difference:

"For the Sadducees say that there is no resurrection, nor angel, nor spirit; but the Pharisees confess all of these."

I read that again. *The Pharisees confess all of these.*

The Pharisees believed in the resurrection of the dead. They believed in angels. They believed in the spirit world. These were the very core tenants of Jesus's own teaching! Theologically, the Pharisees were Jesus's closest allies.

Then I looked at the Sadducees. Acts 5:17 links the high priest and the ruling authorities of the Temple specifically to "the sect of the Sadducees." These were the men in power. These were the ones who denied the existence of the spiritual world Jesus came to reveal.

So, if Jesus was genuinely concerned about spiritual corruption and unbelief, the Sadducees were the obvious target. They controlled the Temple commerce he disrupted. They denied the very resurrection he promised.

Yet, throughout the Gospels, most of Jesus's verbal assaults are targeted at the Pharisees.

When Jesus drove the money changers from the Temple, he was attacking Sadducee territory and Sadducee profits. But when he opened his mouth to condemn "vipers" and "hypocrites" and "sons of hell," he aimed his fire at the Pharisees—the only group that actually agreed with him about the spiritual world.

It was almost as if Jesus had confused the two groups entirely. He directed his harshest criticism at the believers while the actual cynical establishment largely escaped his verbal condemnation.

This realization made Jesus's behavior even more troubling. Was he genuinely unaware of the difference? Or was there something more deliberate at work? Why attack the group closest to your own theology?

Author's Note: *Historical records outside the Bible confirm this oddity and deepen the mystery. History tells us the Sadducees were indeed the wealthy, Roman-collaborating aristocracy who controlled the Temple commerce. The Pharisees, by contrast, were progressive, middle-class reformers who made religion accessible to the common people through the synagogue system. They promoted literacy and flexible interpretation of the law. Historically speaking, a teacher like Jesus would likely have been a Pharisee, or at least their ally.*

These findings raised disturbing questions about Jesus's true motivations for the conflicts he seemed to deliberately provoke.

In any case, from the religious leaders' perspective, whomever they were, Jesus may have looked like every other self-proclaimed spiritual leader: another performer, another rebel.

And he couldn't have been easy to trust. He broke their rules. He veiled his meaning. He refused to answer for himself directly. Most importantly, he claimed to be the king of the Jews, which was an act of treason.

Considering all of this, I'm not sure it's unreasonable to ask for proof. They ask for one miracle to prove he is who he says he is. Jesus performed miracles for nearly every other crowd. Why now did he suddenly claim asking for proof is wrong? He had proven his identity in the past to countless people on numerous occasions.

I was thoroughly confused. I kept reading.

The Pharisees didn't believe Jesus. But they had a legitimate reason to dislike him. Jesus had already publicly shamed them. Repeatedly.

He had driven money changers from the temple, declaring, "Stop turning my Father's house into a market!" (Jn 2:16).

He called them "a brood of vipers." He called them "evil." He called them "hypocrites."

The religious leaders were certainly not innocent. Their actions burdened the people with heavy laws to which they themselves were not subject. They prized appearances over compassion. They enforced tradition over truth.

So, surely, Jesus saw through the veneer. But why pick a fight?

He exposed them. Humiliated them. Publicly. He attacked their reputation.

His teaching to "turn the other cheek" flashed back into my mind. I wondered why he was acting against his stated principles.

I began researching Jesus's insults and what I found caught me off guard.

The insult "offspring of vipers" didn't originate with Jesus. It came directly from John the Baptist, who judged the Pharisees and Sadducees at the Jordan River: "You offspring of vipers, who warned you to flee from the wrath to come?" (Mt 3:7).

Yet later, Jesus uses the exact same terminology. In Matthew 12:34, Jesus says: "You offspring of vipers, how can you, being evil, speak good things?"

And in Matthew 23:27, he escalates the attack: "Woe to you, scribes and Pharisees, hypocrites! For you are like whitened tombs, which outwardly appear beautiful, but inwardly are full of dead men's bones and of all uncleanness."

Jesus's attitude was perplexing. Not only was he apparently picking a fight with the wrong group, but John had also made the very same mistake. Why would they both confront the group that was helping the people? I could find no explanation for this apparent error.

I sat back from the page in contemplation. Their insults were also directed at the scribes. What did Jesus and John have against the scribes? I began researching.

The scribes were the professional copyists and scholars who preserved Jewish religious texts through painstaking hand-copying. In a largely illiterate society, they served as teachers, legal experts, and interpreters of religious law. They held respected positions as the educated class, though they weren't necessarily wealthy like the Sadducees.

Yet both John the Baptist and Jesus attacked them with the same venom they directed at other religious groups. Why target the very people who preserved the scriptures they both quoted?

My guess is this: John's wilderness ministry called for radical repentance and direct relationship with God. From his perspective, the scribes' scholarly interpretations and elaborate traditions might have seemed like unnecessary barriers between people and authentic spiritual experience. But without the scribes, there would be no Hebrew scriptures to reference.

Maybe the scribes represented institutional religious authority through their control of sacred texts and their interpretations. I suppose for prophets, who call people to immediate personal transformation, this scholarly mediation would have felt restrictive. But attacking the preservers of religious tradition while claiming to fulfill that same tradition seems contradictory.

Once again, Jesus and John seemed to be targeting people who were serving important functions in Jewish religious life rather than those who were obviously exploiting the system for personal gain.

Everything felt calculated. But was I reading too much into it?

I remembered Jesus saying: "For with whatever judgment you judge, you will be judged; and with whatever measure you measure, it will be measured to you" (Mt 7:2).

If judgment really does return judgment, as he taught, then wasn't he deliberately sowing these seeds? Didn't he know what would grow from them?

He called them snakes, blind guides, whitewashed tombs. He whipped merchants, flipped tables, and called the temple his domain. These were real provocations.

First was the wedding at Cana, where he seemingly bent himself. Then he walked from town to town performing great miracles for his glory. Now he was contradicting his own teachings about love and judgment, while systematically attacking the very people who were trying to help ordinary Jews while largely ignoring those who exploited them.

None of this makes sense. Why would Jesus behave this way?

Chapter 5

The Performance

As Jesus's reputation grew, so did the crowds, and with them, the weight of expectation. They came not just to hear, but to see, to witness power, to be part of something. Jesus gave them what they came for.

He healed people. He multiplied food. He blew their minds.

But somewhere between the silence of the desert and the roar of the crowd, something had changed.

The scene with Satan in the desert revealed the immense importance of uncompromising integrity. At that time, Jesus resisted Ego by quoting scripture and maintaining his principles.

The stories of Jesus multiplying a few loaves of bread and fish to feed thousands had always inspired me. I thought it showed great compassion and love. Now, however, I was seeing something else.

When Jesus feeds the five thousand, it's easy to frame it as a miracle of compassion. He sees the hunger of the crowd, blesses five loaves and two fish, and somehow it feeds thousands.

But why were thousands there? "A great multitude followed him, because they saw his signs which he did on those who were sick" (Jn 6:2).

They were there because Jesus had been performing public miracles, *repeatedly.* Wasn't this a crowd he'd deliberately cultivated?

He made the blind see, cast out demons, healed lepers with onlookers pressing close. He *performed* again and again, in open daylight, *intentionally.*

At times, he told people to stay silent. But the silence never held. Wouldn't he have known they would talk? Who doesn't talk after being healed of leprosy or blindness? How could you not?

Further, more often than not, Jesus demonstrated where he could not help but be seen. If he truly sought obscurity, why perform at all? And why *in public*?

So even if the feeding itself wasn't intended as spectacle, the crowd's presence was earned through spectacle. I was having trouble reconciling the seeming hypocrisy.

He used divine power in public settings to confirm his identity to the crowds. He drew the crowd through prior spectacle. And he performed in a way that undeniably brought him glory.

The pattern seemed too consistent to be accidental. It appears to be a direct violation of the integrity he demonstrated in the desert, yet what else could I call behavior that seemed to contradict his own teachings about integrity?

Jesus walks across the waves to reach his disciples during a storm. They are terrified. Peter calls out: "Lord, if it's you, tell me to come to you on the water." Jesus says, "Come" (Mt 14:28-29). Peter steps out. He walks. Then sinks.

It's a moment often used to illustrate the need for impeccable faith. But listen to the structure of the request: "If it's you"—it mirrors the voice from the desert that tempted Jesus to test God: "If you are the Son of God."

Jesus refused to jump from the temple's pinnacle to test God; why does he now tempt Peter to take the leap?

Wasn't this the same voice and the same test? What was I seeing?

At this point, my question was no longer: *Was Jesus a man of perfect integrity?*

My question was: Why does he repeatedly contradict himself?

That question unsettles everything that came before. And it changes how I will read everything that comes next.

Shortly after Jesus walked on water, something truly astonishing happened: his own brothers tried to get him arrested. It's not something I have ever heard preached. Have you?

What follows cuts to the heart of one of the greatest contradictions in Jesus's story. You know the popular tale of Mary, the mother of Jesus being visited by the angel Gabriel during her pregnancy?

In that scene, Gabriel proclaims her baby to be the Son of the Most High. Here's what the Gospel of Luke (1:26–38) tells us about Jesus's birth:

An angel named Gabriel appears to Mary and announces that she will conceive and give birth to a son who "will be great and will be called the Son of the Most High. The Lord God will give him the throne of his father David, and he will reign over the house of Jacob forever."

Wait, it says Jesus will reign over the throne of David? That means a political kingship, doesn't it? David was a political ruler. But Jesus never took the physical throne. Was the angel wrong? Was God's will not achieved?

To my mind, either divine omnipotence failed, or the promise was false. I can't find any other way of interpreting this scripture without twisting myself. Can you?

Returning to the conversation between Mary and Gabriel, Mary asks how this is possible since she's a virgin. Gabriel explains that the Holy Spirit will overshadow her, and "the holy one who is born from you will be called the Son of God."

Mary responds with faith: "Behold, the servant of the Lord; let it be done to me according to your word." This story is hard to reconcile with what we see later, because according to scripture, Jesus's entire family, including his mother, thought he was insane.

In fact, scripture suggests Jesus was the shame of the family. It wasn't until after the resurrection that we hear of some family members supporting Jesus's movement.

That brings us back to his brothers betraying Jesus.

Jesus had drawn much attention through public displays of power. So he returned to Galilee, a quieter region. There he encountered his brothers.

To understand what happens next, it's important to know that in that time and place, having an insane family member brought great shame.

Jews of that time thought of insanity as demonic possession. The families of the insane were often shunned, and since survival depended heavily on social bonds, being shunned was very serious.

John 7:1-5 shows the interaction.

When Jesus arrived in Galilee, he encountered his brothers, who knew the authorities were looking to arrest him. But instead of warning him to stay safe, they urged him to go to Judea for the Feast of Booths:

"Depart from here and go into Judea, that your disciples also may see your works which you do. For no one does anything in secret while he seeks to be known openly. If you do these things, reveal yourself to the world."

The Gospel adds this crucial detail: "For even his brothers didn't believe in him."

Whoa! That was a striking conversation. First, his brothers confirm that Jesus's aim is to become a public figure. Second, we find out that they do not believe in him.

Jesus then said to them, "My time has not yet come, but your time is always ready. The world can't hate you, but it hates me, because I testify about it, that its works are evil. You go up to the feast. I am not yet going up to this feast, because my time is not yet fulfilled." He decides to stay in Galilee (Jn 7:6-9).

His brothers must have known the authorities were looking to arrest Jesus, because *everyone knew.* But they urged him to go anyway? Why would your brother want that for you? Jesus had four brothers, and all four shared the same sentiment?

I began tracking down more scripture about his family, and I quickly found a record of their shame in Mark. Jesus had come into a house and "The multitude came together again, so that they could not so much as eat bread. When his friends heard it, they went out to seize him; for they said, 'He is insane'" (Mk 3:20-21).

The WEB translation uses "friends," but that is not how I remembered this passage. I checked the NIV and found "family." I then checked the original Greek (*hoi par' autou*) and found the passage means "those belonging to him." This could mean friends, associates, or family, depending on context.

This is one of the earliest indicators that those closest to Jesus, believed he was mentally unwell. The Greek word for take charge of him (*krateo*) implies physical intervention, the kind one might use for someone in danger of harming themselves.

A few verses later, the confrontation becomes even clearer: "His mother and his brothers came, and standing outside, they sent to him, calling him. A multitude was sitting around him, and they told him, 'Behold, your mother, your brothers, and your sisters are outside looking for you.'

He answered them, 'Who are my mother and my brothers?' Looking around at those who sat around him, he said, 'Behold, my mother and my brothers! For whoever does the will of God is my brother, my sister, and mother'" (Mk 3:31–35).

Based on the fact that they are his family and the fact that Jesus consistently knows people's minds, it's reasonable to assume Jesus knew their intentions. His response gives the strong impression that he disowned his family.

Therefore, when his brothers later try to persuade him to attend the festival, we understand the context. He refuses, saying it is not yet his time.

If you recall, this is not the first time Jesus told someone "No," only to act anyway. Remember the wedding at Cana, when Mary asked him to turn water into wine? He said 'No,' then made the wine.

Here he does it again: "But when his brothers had gone up to the feast, then he also went up, not publicly, but as it were in secret" (Jn 7:10).

The man who taught that the truth sets us free lied to his own family? Which voice lies? Remember, he taught: "Let your 'Yes' be 'Yes' and your 'No' be 'No.' Whatever is more than these is of the evil one." By his own standard, he is of "the evil one."

Then comes this remarkable turn: "The Jews therefore sought him at the feast, and said, 'Where is he?' There was much murmuring among the multitudes concerning him. Some said, 'He is a good man.' Others said, 'Not so, but he leads the multitude astray.' Yet no one spoke openly of him for fear of the Jews" (Jn 7:11–13).

Eventually, Jesus does what he said he would not do: "But when it was now the middle of the feast, Jesus went up into the temple and taught." (Jn 7:14).

Attempts are made to arrest him, but they fail: "So they sought to take him; but no one laid hands on him, because his hour had not yet come" (Jn 7:30).

The implication is mysterious: they couldn't seize him. Why not? Perhaps something held them back? The text is unclear on this point.

Still, deeper questions remain: Why did Jesus lie? I suspect he knew his brothers would turn him in if they knew he was going.

More importantly, I wonder why he went when he had said it was not time.

Even more unsettling: If Mary had truly been visited by an angel proclaiming Jesus as the Son of God, why did she, years later, not support his mission? How could she assume he was insane?

She didn't behave like someone who had been visited by an angel and told her baby was the Son of God, come to save the Jews.

You might have wondered why the genealogies we find in Matthew and Luke are incompatible. So too are the stories of the virgin birth. These appear to be retrofitted to match prophecies and persuade audiences that Jesus was the rightful heir to the throne.

But why?

I suspect these genealogies were included because any educated Jew would not follow him, unless he matched the descriptions of the Messiah as passed down through scripture.

And, if they fabricated the nativity story, it's likely many things were added to Jesus's life story by the writers of Matthew, Mark, Luke, and John to convince us of his divinity and royal lineage.

What's clear is this: the Gospels show that his own family didn't understand or believe him.

Imagine you live in a trailer park and all the generations before you have been working class people of extremely modest means. Now imagine if your son goes around telling people he is the rightful heir to the throne. Imagine him saying he is God in the flesh come to save the nation. Imagine him claiming he can perform miracles.

What would you think?

And that question sparked a realization: think about it ... In Cana, Mary expected Jesus to solve the wine problem and confidently told servants *Do whatever he tells you.* She clearly knew he could perform miracles.

But in other verses Mary behaves as if Jesus is insane, even trying to 'take charge of him' like he's having a mental breakdown.

These stories cannot be true, simultaneously. Can they?

The family betrayal story is deeply embarrassing, so who would invent such unflattering details? Doesn't this suggest it's historical?

The Cana story is flattering and miraculous, which is exactly what you'd expect someone to fabricate to support the idea that Jesus is the Messiah.

I had to step back. My mind was spinning. The contradictions were starting to pile up, and I wasn't completely sure what to make of them.

Author's Note: *A reader might wonder—if Mary later shows up during Jesus's final hours, doesn't this contradict the family rejection narrative? Human psychology is complex. A mother can have serious concerns about her son's mental state while still loving him deeply. Family dynamics often involve this kind of complexity. And, based on what we have seen so far, it's also possible that they fabricated her presence at the crucifixion.*

Chapter 6

Clean Miracles

The pattern of calculated performance was becoming too consistent to be accidental. At this point, a fair-minded detective, or a hopeful reader, must stop and ask: Is this the whole story? What of Jesus's pure, non-egoic actions? We saw one in the story of the woman he saved from stoning. Surely, there must be others.

The question is a vital one. If the divine voice is real, it cannot be a singular event. So, I deliberately paused my investigation into the escalating conflicts to search for it.

The search led me to the healing of the Centurion's servant, which I initially believed was the gold standard for a clean miracle. On the surface, it seems perfect. A Roman centurion asks for help, and Jesus responds.

When he came into Capernaum, a centurion came to him, pleading with him, and saying, "Lord, my servant is lying at home paralyzed, suffering terribly." Jesus said to him, "I will come and heal him."

The centurion answered, "Lord, I am not worthy for you to come under my roof. Just say the word, and my servant will be healed. For I am also a man under authority, having under myself soldiers. I tell this one, 'Go,' and he goes; and to another, 'Come,' and he comes; and to my servant, 'Do this,' and he does it."

When Jesus heard it, he marveled and said to those who followed, "Most certainly I tell you, I have not found so great a faith, not even in Israel. I tell you that many will come from the east and the west, and will sit down with Abraham, Isaac, and Jacob in the Kingdom of Heaven, but the children of the Kingdom will be thrown out into the outer darkness. There will be weeping and gnashing of teeth."

Jesus said to the centurion, "Go your way. Let it be done for you as you have believed." His servant was healed in that hour" (Mt 8:5-13).

On my first several readings, I was convinced this was it. There is no overt spectacle. The healing is performed at a distance. And most importantly, Jesus deflects the glory, marveling at the Centurion's faith. It seemed to be a selfless act.

It was only when one of my early readers pointed out the threat he gave to the Jews and how it didn't feel right that I looked again.

Upon revisiting the passage, I immediately saw it. Buried within this act of compassion is a chilling threat. Jesus declares that "the children of the Kingdom will be thrown out into the outer darkness. There will be weeping and gnashing of teeth."

Why? Because they lack the "so great a faith" that the Centurion possesses. And what is the object of this faith? The Centurion makes it clear: it is faith in Jesus's personal authority to command reality.

So it seems the miracle may not be as clean as I first thought. It reads to me like a backhanded warning: belief *in him* is the new requirement for salvation, and the penalty for wavering faith in him is eternal torment.

Even this most promising candidate for a clean miracle may really be a story about judgment and division.

Do you see it?

This unsettling pattern—where a moment of compassion seems to be used to leverage a threat or build a reputation—appears to be repeated in the healing of the leper. It appears in Mark 1:40-45:

> *A leper came to him, pleading with him, kneeling down to him, and saying to him, "If you want to, you can make me clean."*
>
> *Being moved with compassion, he stretched out his hand, and touched him, and said to him, "I want to. Be made clean." When he had said*

this, immediately the leprosy departed from him, and he was made clean.

He strictly warned him, and immediately sent him out, and said to him, "See that you say nothing to anyone; but go your way, show yourself to the priest, and offer for your cleansing the things which Moses commanded, for a testimony to them."

But he went out, and began to proclaim it much, and to spread the story abroad; so that Jesus could no longer openly enter into a city, but was outside in desert places. They came to him from everywhere.

The initial impulse seems perfectly clean: he was "moved with compassion." This is the divine voice. But then he gives the man a strict command, "See that you say nothing to anyone."

I used to think this was an act of extreme humility and compassion. But now I wonder. How could a man cured of leprosy, a disease that made him a social outcast, possibly remain silent? Wouldn't Jesus, who consistently knows people's minds and hearts, know this command was impossible to follow?

Thinking about it more deeply, I feel the issue is that the Bible explicitly says Jesus knows what's within each person.

John 2:24-25: "But Jesus didn't entrust himself to them, because *he knew everyone,* and because he didn't need for anyone to testify concerning man; for *he himself knew what was in man.*" [emphasis mine]

Further, he claims to be the equal of God (who knows all) multiple times in the New Testament, and if that were true, then he knows what will unfold, just as God does. (We'll discuss his claims of equality with God and the all-knowing nature of God in upcoming chapters).

If he knows the future, then he knows they will not keep quiet. And if he knows that no one can keep quiet after being healed of certain obvious ailments, like leprosy, blindness, death (anyone, even without being a god would know this), then the statement to keep quiet is indicative that he is either not equal to God, as he claims to be (he doesn't see the future as God does), or he is being intentionally deceptive about his aim for glory, which would indicate a lack of integrity.

The result of the man's predictable disobedience was that Jesus's fame exploded. It was a viral marketing campaign. This forces an uncomfortable question: Was the command a genuine desire for obscurity, or a brilliant act of reverse psychology? Was this a "clean" miracle, or was it a performance disguised as a secret?

The pattern repeats itself.

The raising of Jairus's daughter and the healing of the deaf man both begin with a clear move toward privacy, away from the crowd. But both end with the same baffling command to silence that seems engineered to produce the opposite effect. The list of truly clean, uncompromised miracles is shockingly, and revealingly, short. The divine voice was there, but it seems it rarely had the final word.

Let's look to the raising of Jairus's daughter (Mark 5), which provides another powerful example. Jesus throws the crowd of mourners out of the room, taking only his inner circle and the girl's parents inside—a clear attempt to avoid spectacle.

This seems to be a very "clean" setup. But after raising the girl, Mark notes, "He strictly ordered them that no one should know this" (Mk 5:43). The problem is the same as with the leper: How could a family possibly keep the resurrection of their daughter a secret? The command's predictable failure would only serve to amplify his fame.

Another example is the healing of the deaf and mute man (Mark 7). Again, the setup is clean. "He took him aside from the multitude privately" (Mk 7:33). This seems to shows a clear desire to avoid spectacle. But then, after the healing, we see the same pattern: "He commanded them that they should tell no one; but the more he commanded them, so much the more a great deal they proclaimed it" (Mk 7:36).

What about the healing at the Pool of Bethesda (John 5)? On the surface, this one seemed perfect.

Jesus finds a man who has been an invalid for thirty-eight years. The man doesn't ask for healing or even know who Jesus is. Acting with what appears to be pure, unprompted compassion, Jesus simply heals him. The man walks away, not even knowing the name of his benefactor.

It read to me like a completely anonymous, unearned act of grace. Until it wasn't.

Later, the Jewish leaders are furious because the healing was performed on the Sabbath. When they confront Jesus, he has the perfect opportunity to defend his actions on the grounds of pure compassion. But instead of that, he makes one of the most astonishing claims of personal glory in the entire Bible:

"For the Father judges no one, but he has given all judgment to the Son, *that all may honor the Son, even as they honor the Father.* He who doesn't honor the Son doesn't honor the Father who sent him" (John 5:22-23). [emphasis mine]

He had performed a beautiful, anonymous act of healing. But when challenged, he chose not to speak of mercy. Instead, he connected that act directly to a demand that he be honored on the same level as God the Father.

This forced me to ask a difficult question: Was the healing the only goal, or did he also see it as an opportunity to make this claim? What do you think?

Of course, we cannot know what Jesus was truly thinking, but I would like to think that at least saving the woman in the temple from a stoning was the divine voice. And that is precisely what's so troubling—that's all I could find in Jesus's favor.

Author's Note: *During the prepublication process of this book, an early reader pointed out something I had missed, something quite disturbing. He noted that the story of Jesus saving the woman from stoning—the very story that most inspired me as a child—was not in the earliest and most reliable manuscripts of the Bible.*

I investigated my own Bible versions and found, to my dismay, that he was right. My NIV translation contains a stark footnote: "The earliest and most reliable manuscripts and other ancient witnesses do not have John 7:53-8:11."

I was heartbroken. The only story I could find of a pure example of a non-self-serving miracle was, in all likelihood, added by scribes centuries later.

And with that, the harsh realization of this chapter became undeniable. The search for a single, uncompromised miracle in the Gospels had failed. And the one act of pure wisdom and compassion I had clung to was probably not even an original part of the story. It seems there may not be a single, forensically "clean" act of Jesus in the entire Bible.

Chapter 7

The Raising of Lazarus

By now, the momentum is unmistakable. The miracles are growing bolder. The stakes are rising. And Jesus is moving ever closer to Jerusalem. Then comes a moment unlike any before it: the raising of Lazarus.

The Gospel of John tells us that when Lazarus became sick, his sisters sent an urgent message to Jesus. Jesus responded that the sickness was "not to death, but for the glory of God, that God's Son may be glorified by it." Then, despite loving Lazarus and his sisters, Jesus deliberately "stayed two days in the place where he was" (Jn 11:1–6).

I read the passage three times before the contradiction hit me. Each time, I was sure I'd misunderstood something. The text was clear, though: urgent message arrives; Jesus announces Lazarus won't die, then waits for *two days*. While his friend suffers.

I turned off my monitor and slumped in disappointment. This wasn't the Jesus I thought I knew.

Lazarus is dying. His sisters send an urgent message. Jesus receives the message, and he waits—*Two more days!*

I had to go for a walk to digest this.

When I returned, I reread the passage, and my mind stuck on this: *"This sickness is not to death, but for the glory of God, that God's Son may be glorified by it."* [emphasis mine]

Glory? Again? Jesus then told his disciples that Lazarus had "fallen asleep," but when they misunderstood this as literal sleep, he clarified: "Lazarus is dead. I am glad for your sakes that I was not there, so that you may believe. Nevertheless, let's go to him" (Jn 11:11-15).

For your sake I am glad I was not there. My stomach knotted.

He's *glad* his friend died. Because now he can perform a bigger miracle, a more spectacular demonstration? Which voice seeks glory at the expense of their friend and his family's suffering?

I thought about my own friendships. If someone I loved was dying and I had the power to save them, how could I delay? How could I be *glad* they suffered so I could look more impressive?

The story continues with Jesus's arrival at Bethany (Jn 11:17-26).

When Jesus arrived, he found that Lazarus had been in the tomb four days already. When Martha heard that Jesus was coming, she along with many others went out to meet him.

Martha said to Jesus, "Lord, if you would have been here, my brother wouldn't have died. Even now I know that whatever you ask of God, God will give you." Jesus said to her, "Your brother will rise again." He continued: "I am the resurrection and the life. He who believes in me will still live, even if he dies. Whoever lives and believes in me will never die. Do you believe this?" (Jn 11:25-26)

He's coercing them to proclaim *his* identity, using their grief? Which voice is focused on glorifying identity?

I felt sick.

When Jesus saw Mary and the others weeping, he was deeply moved and asked where they had laid Lazarus. They led him to the tomb, and Jesus wept. (Jn 11:33-35)

He weeps? The man who deliberately delayed for effect while their brother died now weeps at their grief? Who says they are glad in private, then weeps in public?

Some of those present mirrored my doubt about Jesus's integrity: They said, "Couldn't this man, who opened the eyes of him who was blind, have also kept this man from dying?" (Jn 11:37)

Many of us are so inspired by miraculous power and the beauty of some of Jesus's teachings, that we overlook the fact that Jesus could have prevented this death in the first place. Up until this book project, that was me. But the conscience of those who are not so wooed speaks up.

Maybe we are not so different from the people in those days.

Jesus went to the tomb and commanded those present to take away the stone blocking the entrance. He then lifted up his eyes, and said, "Father, I thank you that you listened to me. I know that you always listen to me, but because of the multitude standing around I said this, that they may believe that you sent me." Then in a loud voice, he cried out "Lazarus, come out!" (Jn 11:38-43).

Wait. *"I said this for the benefit of the people standing here"?* Did I read that right? Isn't he suggesting that his prayer is a performance? Is even his communication with God staged for the crowd?

Which voice stages conversations with God? Which voice turns even prayer into theater?

For the first time, I found myself completely repelled by the man in this story.

And then I remembered: Jesus himself taught *not* to pray in public: "When you pray, you shall not be as the hypocrites, for they love to stand and pray in the synagogues and in the corners of the streets, that they may be seen by men" (Mt 6:5).

But here he was, staging his prayer for maximum public impact, and with far greater flair than the Pharisees he condemned! Am I hallucinating?

Yet somehow, Lazarus walked out. *Alive.*

Jesus delayed intentionally. He stated that the purpose was to glorify God—*and himself.* And from what I can see, he fully orchestrated the moment.

What's happening here?

The language he uses—"so that God's Son may be glorified through it"—the word *glory* again. That's the tell, isn't it?

In the desert, he refused to bow to gain the kingdoms. But here, he orchestrates a death to gain glory. *Is this the same man?*

Jesus said he waited two days so that others might believe. He intentionally allowed Lazarus to suffer and die. And he did it to *glorify himself.*

It may be tempting to think this is just opinion or speculation, but the Bible clearly tells us he did it for his glory. Thus, any argument on this point is against the explicit text found in *every version of the Bible.*

If this had been your brother, your sister, your child; If you had watched them gasp and struggle and slip away, only to find out that the one you called for help, the one who could have spared them delayed on purpose, to make a spectacle of their return—wouldn't you have called it cruel?

Everything in me wanted to be done with this project. But I couldn't. Not if I was going to maintain integrity and honor my promise to Jesus. Why did I still feel I needed to honor that promise? For some reason, I felt I must.

At this point, I asked myself this question that I will now pose to you: Having examined these instances—the moments of apparent deception, the actions seemingly driven by a desire for glory even at the cost of others' distress, the harsh judgments that stand in contrast to calls for love, the deliberate obscuring of truth, do you trust this man?

If these were the actions of any other individual, any leader, any friend, any spiritual guide we encountered today, and we held them to the simple ethical standards we expect in our daily lives, the standards many of us were taught as children, perhaps even the very standards often espoused as 'Christian values'— would you trust such a person?

Would you entrust them with your deepest concerns, your well-being, or the well-being of your loved ones? Your children?

And if you would trust him, could you at least understand why another person might not?

I sat with this question as I continued reading, knowing I had to follow the evidence wherever it led.

Jesus had to know that this miracle would seal his fate, for it would surely spread the word among the masses that he was the king of the Jews, and that assertion was a direct challenge to Herod and Rome.

Scripture confirms this: many who witnessed the miracle believed in him, but others reported what Jesus had done to the Pharisees. The chief priests and Pharisees gathered a council, worried that if they left Jesus alone, "everyone will believe in him, and the Romans will come and take away both our place and our nation" (Jn 11:48).

Caiaphas, the high priest, made the calculation explicit: "It is advantageous for us that one man should die for the people, and that the whole nation not perish" (Jn 11:50). From that day forward, they plotted to kill him.

Any surge of popular messianic fervor could trigger a violent Roman crackdown. The consequences could be devastating for the entire population.

Maybe the Jewish leaders weren't simply scheming. They were navigating a fragile peace under brutal occupation, with everything at stake. Obviously, Jesus stepped into it, deliberately.

This miracle raised the temperature to a boil, and it put Jesus on the cross.

Author's Note: *I need to pause here for a moment, because what the text is showing us is profoundly disturbing. If you feel a sense of revulsion or disbelief, I understand. I felt the same way. It is at this exact point that our minds will desperately search for a "why"—a deeper theological reason, a psychological explanation, or a way to give the benefit of the doubt—to soften this horrifying conclusion.*

This impulse is a testament to our desire to see the good Jesus, whom we believe we know. We want to believe in a hero. We want the story to be about love, not this. I ask you only to stay with the uncomfortable feeling for a moment, and to honor it, without trying to explain it away. The purpose of this investigation is not to prove a point, but to see what happens when we commit to looking at the "what"—what is actually written on the page, and what are its implications—before we rush to find a "why." The difficult truth of the text and its implications must be seen clearly before anything else is possible.

For our investigation, I ask you to simply sit with the "what" for a moment: the text says he delayed for glory while his friends suffered. Acknowledging the plain meaning of the text is the first step.

Interlude:

Crucifixion

Have you ever wondered why Jesus told people to "take up your cross and follow me"? I had always glossed over this statement, not realizing just what he meant. What I found through my research added a lot of depth to my reading experience with the Gospels.

When Jesus told his followers to "take up your cross," his Jewish audience would have understood exactly what he meant. Modern readers may need context to grasp the full horror of what he was asking.

Crucifixion was Rome's most degrading form of execution, reserved for slaves, rebels, and criminals deemed unworthy of a swift death. Roman citizens were exempt—no matter their crime, they could not be crucified. This alone tells us how the practice was viewed.

The Roman class system emerges clearly through crucifixion's restrictions—citizens were exempt regardless of crime, marking it as punishment for the "unworthy." This reveals how Romans viewed non-citizens as fundamentally different categories of human beings.

For Jews, this denial of burial had even more terrifying theological implications. Jewish belief held that on the Day of Judgment, God would establish justice on earth and raise the righteous dead in physical, bodily resurrection to participate in the restored kingdom.

Scripture promised: "Many of those who sleep in the dust of the earth shall awake, some to everlasting life" (Daniel 12:2). Bodies needed to be preserved for this physical resurrection.

From a Jewish perspective, crucifixion was far more than just execution—it was eternal annihilation. The crucified would be marked as cursed by God, denied resurrection, and excluded forever from the world to come.

The condemned carried their own crossbeam through the streets while crowds hurled insults and debris. Once at the execution site, they were stripped naked and nailed or tied to the cross. Death came slowly, sometimes taking days, as victims struggled to breathe while their body weight pulled down on their pierced arms.

But the physical agony was only part of the punishment. Crucifixion was designed as public theater. Bodies were displayed along busy roads where travelers could see them—a warning about the consequences of defying Rome. The humiliation was intentional and complete.

For Jews, crucifixion carried additional horror. Deuteronomy 21:23 declared that "anyone hung on a tree is under God's curse." A crucified person was marked as personally rejected by God. The shame extended to their entire family, who would carry the stigma for generations.

This makes Jesus's teaching even more radical. He was asking followers to embrace what Jewish theology taught would damn them eternally, while promising that this very path—crucifixion—would somehow lead to eternal life. This represented a complete inversion of Jewish beliefs about salvation and damnation.

Worse still, Roman authorities typically left bodies on crosses for days or weeks, letting them rot and become food for scavengers. Jewish law required burial on the same day to avoid defiling the land, but Rome often deliberately denied this basic dignity.

Families couldn't properly mourn, couldn't perform burial rites, couldn't honor their dead. The degradation continued long after death, because failure to bury the intact body meant the person could not rise to life on the day of resurrection.

So, when Jesus said, "take up your cross," he wasn't speaking metaphorically or about wearing a cross necklace. That practice didn't begin until well after Jesus died. He was asking his followers to prepare for the most shameful death imaginable—one that would mark them as cursed by God, dishonor their families, and potentially deny them proper burial.

Jesus himself provided the paradoxical logic for this reversal, teaching that the only way to gain true life was to lose the life of the self:

"For whoever wants to save his life will lose it; and whoever will lose his life for my sake and the sake of the Good News will save it" (Mark 8:35).

It seems Jesus knew they would die an agonizing, shameful death, as did his followers and their families. Can you imagine how you might feel about a family member following a preacher like that knowing the consequences? What would you say or even do to such a family member to prevent that outcome?

This might be part of the reason Jesus's family called him insane and tried to get him arrested in Judea, and then personally try to "take hold of him" when he managed to escape arrest.

It may also give new context to Jesus's prediction that he had come to bring "a sword" between family members. When following Jesus meant preparing for crucifixion, families faced desperate choices. Historical evidence suggests some early Christian families did resort to violence to prevent their loved ones from pursuing such a path.

It's just a guess, but perhaps this explains Jesus's extreme instruction that followers must "hate" their families and even themselves. If joining his movement meant inevitable family conflict and social pressure to abandon the path to crucifixion, complete emotional detachment might be the only way to follow through.

The cross meant far more than individual martyrdom—it meant severing every bond that might prevent someone from accepting the most shameful death possible.

Chapter 8

The Ultimate Stage

After Lazarus walked out of that tomb, Jesus turned toward Jerusalem, having proven that death is not the final frontier. Now it was time to prove the same thing to Rome.

The crowd that once whispered his name now shouted it. Palm branches waved. Cloaks were thrown on the ground. The people cried: "Hosanna! Blessed is he who comes in the name of the Lord!" (Mk 11:19).

He rode in on a donkey. Wait—wasn't there a prophecy about this? The Messiah coming on a donkey? I checked, and sure enough, Jesus was performing it exactly.

"Rejoice greatly, daughter of Zion! Shout, daughter of Jerusalem! Behold, your King comes to you! He is righteous, and having salvation; lowly, and riding on a donkey, even on a colt, the foal of a donkey" (Zech 9:9).

But wasn't this earlier text about a political king who would bring peaceful restoration to Jerusalem after the Babylonian exile some 500 years before Jesus was born? Did Jesus think that prophecy referred to him?

In any case, Jesus orchestrated it precisely. He even told the disciples where to find the animal: "saying to them, 'Go your way into the village that is opposite you, and immediately you will find a donkey tied, and a colt with her. Untie them and bring them to me'" (Mt 21:2).

This had to be a message. But to whom, and for what purpose?

To the crowds chanting "Hosanna," this was a coronation, it seems. To the Romans, it must have been a provocation. And to the Pharisees, a threat.

He entered the city as a king. And they all responded accordingly.

By this point, I had become numb to his provocations. Of course he orchestrated it. Of course it was theater.

He walks into the temple. He sees the commerce, the money changers. He hears the noise. And he overturns the tables. He drives them out. "It is written, 'My house shall be called a house of prayer,' but you have made it a 'den of robbers!'" (Mt 21:13).

He calls the temple *his house*, as if Jerusalem is his kingdom.

More theater. I could see it now, the carefully orchestrated anger, the strategic table-flipping, the perfectly timed declarations. Even his rage was a performance.

But the consequences were real. In occupied Jerusalem, claiming the temple as your house was treason. Performance or not, heads were going to roll for this. Jesus knew it.

Then he teaches. He heals. He confronts. He is pressing forward into the eye of the storm. The more he reveals, the more the opposition gathers: Pharisees, Priests, Roman authorities.

This cannot stand. He is too public, too bold, too dangerous.

A plot begins. One of his own will betray him. The wheels are turning.

Jesus gathers with his disciples in an upper room to share the Passover. They sit together, reclining at the table. The bread, the wine, the ritual—all familiar elements of a sacred meal.

But something is different. A heaviness hangs in the room. "He said to them, 'I have earnestly desired to eat this Passover with you before I suffer'" (Lk 22:15).

"He took bread, gave thanks and broke it, and gave it to them, saying, 'This is my body which is given for you. Do this in memory of me'" (Lk 22:19).

Then after supper, he took a cup of wine and declared a new covenant in his blood, poured out for his disciples.

"Most certainly, I tell you, unless you eat the flesh of the Son of Man and drink his blood, you don't have life in yourselves. He who eats my flesh and drinks my blood has eternal life, and I will raise him up at the last day. For my flesh is food indeed, and my blood is drink indeed" (Jn 6:53–55).

I sat back in my chair, stunned. Jesus was telling his followers to spiritually eat his flesh and drink his blood. Even as symbolic ritual, this was staggering.

And then I understood what this would have meant to any Jew of that time.

To the Jews, consuming blood was one of the most forbidden acts possible, strictly prohibited by Levitical law: "For the life of the flesh is in the blood. I have given it to you on the altar to make atonement for your souls; for it is the blood that makes atonement by reason of the life. Therefore I have said to the children of Israel, 'No person among you may eat blood, nor may any stranger who lives as a foreigner among you eat blood'" (Lv 17:14).

And eating human flesh, even symbolically? That would be the ultimate abomination. From any Jewish perspective, he was instructing his followers to perform what would be seen as an idolatrous sacrament that violated their most sacred laws. No wonder the religious leaders were so horrified by him.

Then Jesus says what no one expects: "Most certainly I tell you, one of you will betray me—one who is eating with me" (Jn 13:21).

The disciples are stunned. Each begins to ask: *Surely you don't mean me?*

As I kept reading, I found something that stopped me cold. Let me share what Jesus had said earlier that evening: 'I know whom I have chosen. But that the Scripture might be fulfilled, "He who eats bread with me has lifted up his heel against me."' (Jn 13:18).

I looked up the quoted scripture and found it comes from Psalm 41:9: "Yes, my own familiar friend, in whom I trusted, who ate my bread, has lifted up his heel against me."

It's about King David lamenting that his trusted companion betrayed him. It has nothing to do with Jesus. But Jesus was using this scripture to refer to Judas, who would betray him. "I know whom I have chosen" (Jn 13:18). Jesus chose Judas, knowing he would betray him?!

"But that the word may be fulfilled that is written in their law, 'They hated me without a cause.' I am telling you now before it happens, so that when it does happen you will believe that I am who I am" (Jn 13:18–19).

He's planning this betrayal to fulfill prophecy—that isn't really prophecy? And he tells them ahead of time so they'll believe who he is?

"Most certainly, I tell you, he who receives whomever I send receives me, and he who receives me receives him who sent me" (Jn 13:20).

It seems like he has prepared this scene, so he could assert his divine authority, again.

Then Jesus repeated that one of his disciples would betray him. When asked who, he said it would be the one to whom he gave the dipped bread. "So when he had dipped the piece of bread, he gave it to Judas, the son of Simon Iscariot. After the piece of bread, then Satan entered into him. Then Jesus said to him, 'What you do, do quickly'" (Jn 13:21-27).

Doesn't this mean Jesus not only knew who would betray him, but that he orchestrated it? He dipped the bread. He handed it to Judas. And the moment Judas took it, Satan entered into him.

How had I not noticed this before? Doesn't it seem like Jesus infected Judas with Satan?

Then he gave the order: "What you are about to do, do quickly" (Jn 13:27).

And Judas immediately leaves the table, to do exactly what Jesus had just compelled him to do.

It reads to me as if Jesus manufactured his betrayer. As if he programmed Judas through implantation, then commanded him to act. So that he could prove he was the Son of God.

I struggled to see how Jesus could be innocent in this. It's the ultimate entrapment, is it not? Entrapment happens when police coerce someone into committing a crime and then arrest them for it.

I couldn't believe that the Bible so clearly shows Jesus forcing Judas to betray him, but I couldn't read it any other way. I felt utter *revulsion*. It's nothing like we have been taught. For two thousand years Christians have judged Judas as a betrayer, but Judas may not have had a choice in the matter.

Jesus retreats to the garden. He brings a few disciples to watch over him as he prays alone: "Father, if it is possible, let this cup pass from me. Yet not my will, but Yours be done" (Mt 26:39).

The soldiers, guided by Judas, come to arrest Jesus. Judas kisses Jesus to signal the soldiers.

They attempt to arrest Jesus, but Peter draws his sword and cuts off a soldier's ear. Jesus stops him from further violence: "Put your sword back into its place, for all those who take the sword will die by the sword" (Mt 26:52).

Jesus heals the soldier's ear. Then they arrest Jesus and drag him from the garden in the dead of night.

First, they take him to the high priest, where accusations swirl and witnesses contradict each other. He is silent.

The Priests demand: "Are you the Messiah, the Son of the Blessed One?" "Jesus said, 'I am. You will see the Son of Man sitting at the right hand of Power, and coming with the clouds of the sky'" (Mk 14:61–62).

At this, they accuse him of blasphemy. He is beaten, spat upon, and mocked.

I had always read this passage without question, but now I recognized that I didn't really know what drove the Priests into such a rage. I began my research.

To modern readers like me, Jesus's response might seem like a simple affirmation, but to his Jewish audience, these words carried devastating implications.

First, we must understand the question. When the High Priest asked if he was the "Son of God," he wasn't asking if Jesus was divine. In the Old Testament, "Son of God" was a royal title given to the King of Israel (Psalm 2:7). The Priest was asking a political question: "Are you claiming to be the King?"

Jesus's response, however, escalated the claim from political to cosmic. By declaring "I am," Jesus echoed God's sacred self-identification to Moses as "I AM WHO I AM" (Ex 3:14)—the divine name. Jesus was calling himself God.

To the priests, his reference to the "Son of Man" wasn't humble self-description but an invocation of Daniel's apocalyptic vision, where a divine figure receives eternal dominion over all nations.

The phrase "sitting at the right hand of Power" claimed a share in God's very throne, while "coming with the clouds" appropriated imagery reserved exclusively for divine beings in Jewish scripture.

The high priest understood immediately: Jesus wasn't merely claiming to be the Messiah, a human king they could accept or reject. He was claiming equality with God himself.

In their religious framework, this was the ultimate blasphemy, a violation of the fundamental principle of monotheism that demanded death. The beating and mockery that followed weren't random cruelty but the prescribed response to someone who had, in their view, committed the most serious offense possible against the divine order.

They then order that Jesus be taken to Pilate, the Roman Governor. Pilate has no interest in charges of blasphemy. His interest is in Jesus's claim to be a king.

Pilate said to him, "Are you a king then?" Jesus answered, "You say that I am a king. For this reason I have been born, and for this reason I have come into the world, that I should testify to the truth. Everyone who is of the truth listens to my voice" (Lk 23:3). He says nothing more.

Pilate is puzzled. He questions, prods, and even sends him to Herod Antipas, who ruled over Galilee and Perea. But Jesus still will not defend himself.

If Jesus claimed to be the king of the Jews to Pilate or Herod, they would have sentenced him to crucifixion, but Jesus remained silent.

He is brought back to the crowd to decide his fate. But, the crowd has turned against him, due to the chief priests' accusations.

They chant, "Crucify him!" (Mk 15:13)

Pilate pleads to spare Jesus. He even offers to release a prisoner to appease them, but the people choose to save Barabbas, a known criminal, over Jesus.

Again, Jesus does not defend himself. They beat him. Mock him. Crown him with thorns. And they nail him to the cross.

"If you are the Son of God, come down from the cross!" tease the Roman soldiers. (Mt 27:40)

Something about this scene felt familiar. Hadn't Satan tempted Jesus to throw himself from the temple, to see if God would send his angels to save him? But God does not call down angels to protect him.

Jesus hangs. He bleeds. He suffers.

At the ninth hour, he cries out: "My God, my God, why have you forsaken me?" (Mt 27:46)

I paused. Something about that phrase was nagging at me. Where had I read those words before?

I looked it up. Psalm 22:1. Word for word. I was surprised to see just how tightly Psalm 22 (written by King David centuries earlier) matches the crucifixion scene:

The Psalm *(22:7-8)* describes a mocking crowd that matches the behavior of the priests and crowd toward Jesus in Matthew 27:39-43. *Psalm (22:16) reads,* "For dogs have surrounded me. A company of evildoers have enclosed me. They have pierced my hands and feet." Doesn't this describe Jesus's crucifixion?

The Psalm (22:18) describes how they divide his garments among them and cast lots (gambled) for his clothing, which matches the Roman soldiers casting lots for Jesus's tunic (Jn 19:24).

Then there is the thirst. The Psalm (22:15) reads, "My tongue sticks to the roof of my mouth." Jesus calls back to it with "I thirst" (Jn 19:28).

Then I learned that in Jewish tradition, quoting the opening line of a Psalm (like a song title) invokes the entire text. By crying out the first verse of **Psalm 22**, Jesus wasn't just expressing pain; he was effectively telling the Jewish audience, "Go read the script. I am acting this out right now."

Even on the cross, in the midst of the ultimate torture, he was performing! The psalm was David's personal lament about his own persecution and enemies.

The soldiers offer him wine vinegar. I looked it up. It's another echo of King David's lament. "They gave me vinegar for my thirst" (Ps 69:21).

Then he said: "Father, forgive them, for they do not know what they are doing" (Lk 23:34).

The irony hit me unexpectedly. The man who had systematically planned and provoked these very people into crucifying him was forgiving them?

Finally, he said: "It is finished." He breathed his last (Jn 19:30).

What had I just witnessed? I felt I had to be missing something.

Wait ... If Jesus orchestrated his own crucifixion through systematic provocation, as the Gospel accounts clearly show, if the Jewish leaders really had no choice, due to the impossible pressure they were under, then why have the Jews taken the blame as "Christ-killers" for two thousand years?

Jesus had a cleaner option. If Jesus simply wanted to be crucified, he could have told Pilate he was the King of the Jews. Pilate would have executed him for treason, and Rome would have borne the blame. But he didn't do that. He refused to answer Pilate, forcing the Jews to demand his death. You see? He engineered his death *and the blame.*

This supposed guilt has been the excuse for pogroms (violent mob attacks) across Russia and Eastern Europe, forced conversions throughout Medieval Europe, expulsions from England, France, Spain, ghettoization and legal restrictions, and ultimately, the Holocaust. Millions of Jews have suffered unimaginably and died.

If God is omniscient, as 1 John 3:20 insists: "God is greater than our hearts, and he knows everything," then Jesus as God would not be the savior of the Jewish people. He would be their greatest enemy.

Author's Note: *I know how difficult this logical extrapolation is to consider. The impulse to think this is an out-of-bounds conclusion because Jesus's motivation is not explicitly stated in the biblical texts is understandable. But we do not need to have everything spelled out. We have all the evidence necessary to justify this conclusion, even if our sentimentality doesn't like it. It's what a detective must do to conduct an honest investigation.*

Please understand, this is not an emotional accusation. It is the result of a simple, but brutal, logical sequence based on the story's own rules: If the character of Jesus is presented as omniscient God, then he must have known the consequences of his meticulously engineered crucifixion. This is about holding a character who claims divine foresight accountable for the foreseeable outcome of his own actions. It is a horrifying "what" that we must look at clearly, without flinching.

Chapter 9

The People's Court

In contemplation, my mind returned to the scene immediately leading up to Jesus's judgement and crucifixion. What were the elders doing while Jesus was being interrogated by Pilate and Herod?

The Gospels mention they "stirred up the crowd" (Mark 15:11) and "persuaded the crowd" (Matthew 27:20) to demand Barabbas and condemn Jesus.

Author's Note: *To understand the trial, we must understand the two men who held the power of life and death over Jesus. They were not merely religious figures but rival politicians navigating a powder keg.*

Pontius Pilate *was the Roman Governor (Prefect) of Judea. He was the only man with the legal authority to order a crucifixion. Historically, he was known for his cruelty and stubbornness, often provoking the Jews by displaying Roman idols. The Gospel portrayal of him as a "reluctant, sympathetic judge" is a stark contradiction to the historical record.*

Herod Antipas *was the client King ruling over Galilee (where Jesus was from), on behalf of Rome. He was the son of Herod the Great (who is known for ordering the massacre of the innocents). Antipas is the one who beheaded John the Baptist. He had no authority in Jerusalem, but Pilate sent Jesus to him to possibly pass the buck and avoid a riot.*

I imagined the scene, based on the evidence the Jewish leaders had against Jesus.

While Jesus stood before Pilate in private interrogation, outside in the courtyard a different trial was taking place. The religious authorities addressed the gathering crowd with urgent purpose.

"People of Jerusalem," calls out Caiaphas, his voice carrying authority, "you have followed this man for his miracles and teachings. But we must warn you of the danger he poses to our very survival."

The crowd quiets, sensing the gravity of the moment.

"This man claims to be King of the Jews while Caesar rules," Caiaphas continues, gesturing toward the Praetorium. "Even now he stands before Pilate. If Rome hears of a rival king among us, legions will descend upon Jerusalem. Remember what they did to other cities that harbored rebels."

Murmurs of concern ripple through the crowd. They knew Roman brutality.

An elder steps forward: "But his threat goes beyond politics. When we questioned by whose authority he performs these signs, he refused to answer directly. A true prophet of God gives glory to the Almighty. This man conceals his source of power."

"Worse still," Caiaphas's voice rises, "he claims equality with God himself. When challenged, he declared: 'Before Abraham was, I AM'—taking upon himself the sacred name that Moses heard at the burning bush."

Gasps echo through the assembly. This was unmistakable blasphemy.

"He threatened to destroy our holy temple," another elder adds, "claiming he would rebuild it in three days. This sanctuary where your fathers worshipped, where you bring your children—he would tear it down!"

Caiaphas raises his hand: "One who was closest to him has more to reveal. This man handled their money, heard their secret teachings."

He gestures to Judas, who steps forward.

"I am Judas Iscariot, son of Simon. For three years I walked with Jesus of Nazareth as one of his twelve chosen disciples."

Several in the crowd nod recognition.

"I speak from duty to our people and to the truth God requires." Judas's voice carries across the courtyard: "He commands his followers to drink his blood and eat his flesh, saying we cannot have eternal life without consuming him. You

56

know the Law—even animal blood is forbidden, yet he demands we drink human blood."

The crowd recoils in horror. This violated their deepest religious taboos.

"He identifies himself with the bronze serpent that Moses lifted in the wilderness—the very image of the plague that was killing our ancestors. He compares himself to that accursed idol, demanding we look upon him for salvation."

"He claims authority to judge the living and the dead," Judas continues. "Those who don't believe in him, he says, will face eternal fire. Not temporary punishment—eternal torment for not accepting him as divine."

"Abomination!" someone shouts. Others join. The crowd's understanding transforms.

Caiaphas steps forward one final time: "This man seeks not to serve God, but to replace Him. His hidden teachings violate everything Moses gave us. We must choose: preserve our covenant with the true God, or follow this blasphemer to destruction. What say you?"

The crowd that had shouted "Hosanna" days before now saw a different figure—one whose claims threatened both their theology and their survival.

A voice rings out: "Crucify him!" Another echoes it. Soon the entire courtyard thunders with unified condemnation: "Crucify! Crucify!"

When Pilate finally emerged with Jesus, the verdict had already been sealed in the people's hearts.

Of course, this is just what I imagined must have happened. What do you think?

Chapter 10

The Resurrection

I resumed reading, and I found something even more puzzling in Matthew's account.

According to Matthew, "At that moment the curtain of the temple was torn in two from top to bottom. The earth shook, the rocks split and the tombs broke open. The bodies of many holy people who had died were raised to life. They came out of the tombs after Jesus's resurrection and went into the holy city and appeared to many people" (Mt 27:51-53).

A zombie apocalypse in Jerusalem? Dead saints walking around the city?

I had to laugh at the mental image. Picture the scene: You're a Roman centurion doing your rounds when suddenly Grandpa Moses shambles past, asking for directions to the temple. Do you file a report? Call for backup? Pretend you didn't see anything?

I checked Mark. Nothing. Luke. Nothing. John. Complete silence.

How do three Gospel writers miss what would have been the most sensational event in human history? How do Roman historians, who documented every earthquake and eclipse, somehow overlook the day the dead took a stroll through their occupied capital city?

For the life of me, I can't figure out how I had missed this in my previous readings. Zombies? I felt like someone added that when I wasn't looking.

I sat back, incredulous. These are supposed to be eyewitness accounts of the most important event in human history, and they can't agree on the basic facts? Who was there, what they saw, what they did?

But here's what really got me—each Gospel writer swears they're telling the truth. Luke claims he carefully investigated everything. John insists we know that his testimony is true. They all present themselves as reliable witnesses.

Yet they contradict each other on details any actual witness would remember clearly. For example, after they place Jesus in the tomb, did Mary later visit his body alone or with others? Was there one angel or two inside? Did they tell anyone or stay silent?

We are in fact reading four completely different stories, each claiming to be the definitive account of the same event.

Now, to be fair, this zombie scenario might not have seemed as absurd to Matthew's original audience. Both Jews and early Christians expected a literal resurrection of the dead on the Day of Judgment. In Jewish eschatology, the righteous dead would rise bodily when the Messiah established God's kingdom.

Matthew may have been suggesting that Jesus's death triggered the final resurrection that the Jews long expected. To the Jews, resurrected saints walking around Jerusalem would have seemed like the natural fulfillment of prophecy rather than a supernatural horror movie.

And, of course, the holy dead rising at the moment of Jesus's death would be definitive proof Jesus was the true Messiah. And isn't that the point of the zombie scene?

But here's the problem: if this was such a significant theological moment—the beginning of the general resurrection that Jews had been anticipating for centuries, why didn't the other Gospel writers mention it? Why didn't Paul reference it in his detailed discussions of resurrection? Why don't we find any mention of it in early church writings?

The silence is deafening.

Next we have the resurrection accounts themselves. And here, something remarkable happened. Jesus didn't just appear as a spirit or vision. According to Matthew, Luke, and John, he went out of his way to prove his body was physical.

Jesus tells his frightened disciples: "Look at my hands and my feet. It is I myself! Touch me and see; a ghost does not have flesh and bones, as you see I have" (Lk 24:39).

He ate fish in front of them. He let Thomas touch his wounds. He walked and talked and prepared breakfast on the beach.

And then Jesus was taken up into heaven like Elijah—alive.

Author's Note: *You might note that Matthew, Luke, and John share detailed accounts of Jesus rising, but the oldest versions of Mark, which is the earliest recorded Gospel, contain no mention of the resurrection. Mark originally ended at 16:8 with women fleeing the empty tomb in fear and telling no one. The resurrection appearances in Mark 16:9-20 were added by later scribes. It's the ultimate moment of Jesus's mission. All of Christianity depends on the resurrection—and Mark omits it?*

While most modern Bibles include the longer ending (verses 9-20), they typically mark it with brackets or footnotes stating it is missing from the oldest and most reliable manuscripts. This provides strong evidence that the Gospels are not accurate reflections of Jesus's ministry. That said, this book tracks the narrative story of Jesus as we have inherited it, which includes Matthew's zombies and may or may not include Jesus's resurrection depending on which version of Mark you read.

What do you think of these overt discrepancies?

Part II

The Unveiling

In Part I, we undertook the difficult task of creating an accurate map. We looked at the character of Jesus as he is presented in the Gospels and, holding him to his own stated standards, documented the terrain of his words and actions. We noted the contradictions, the moments of hypocrisy, and the unsettling patterns without looking away. We now have our collection of clues.

Now, in Part II, "The Unveiling," our investigation takes a crucial turn. We will move from simply documenting these clues to asking what they mean when viewed together. If the inconsistencies are the fingerprints left at the scene, now we must ask: whose fingerprints are they? We will begin to connect these seemingly random data points to see if they form a single, coherent signature.

Before we continue, I need to be honest with you. In this next stage of our investigation, the path gets steeper. As we move from observing contradictions to interpreting the pattern they create, the conclusions become even more challenging.

I know this because my own mind fought this next step tooth and nail. While writing this section, every instinct I had was to find an escape route—to reach for a historical explanation, a psychological theory from someone like Jung, or a more comfortable theological interpretation that would soften the blow. Many of my early readers reported this same struggle. But if we do that, we will be doing what everyone has done for millennia, and miss seeing what's been hiding right there in the text for just as long.

Let's commit once more to being detectives together, focusing only on the evidence presented in the text and Jesus's own stated standards.

Chapter 11

The Veil

Considering the massive discrepancies between the Gospels regarding the crucifixion and resurrection, I had to wonder whether Jesus's followers weren't completely blindsided when Jesus died and did not resurrect.

Reading the Gospels, it's clear his disciples didn't understand that Jesus was aiming for crucifixion, even though he told them of his aim multiple times. And if they heard him, they clearly did not believe he would actually die.

The evidence was right there in passages I'd read dozens of times but never really seen: "After Jesus had been with his disciples for some time, teaching, healing, and performing miracles, he began to speak more plainly about what lay ahead: saying, 'The Son of Man must suffer many things, and be rejected by the elders, chief priests, and scribes, and be killed, and the third day be raised up'" (Lk 9:22).

Peter, who had just proclaimed Jesus to be the Messiah, rebukes his true aim: 'Far be it from you, Lord! This will never be done to you' (Mt 16:22).

Jesus responds with stunning force: "Get behind me, Satan! You are a stumbling block to me, for you are not setting your mind on the things of God, but on the things of men" (Mt 16:23).

According to the narrative, it was God's will that he be killed and raised up, but they couldn't see it, even when he said it plainly.

Mark records Jesus more explicitly: "for he was teaching his disciples, and said to them, 'The Son of Man is being handed over to the hands of men, and they will kill him; and when he is killed, on the third day he will rise again'" (Mk 9:31).

Luke 9:45 echoes the same moment but adds something: "But they didn't understand this saying. It was concealed from them, that they should not perceive it, and they were afraid to ask him about this saying" (Lk 9:45).

Concealed? By whom? And for what purpose? The text offers no immediate answer, but the question itself hangs over the rest of the narrative.

Luke continues: "Then an argument started among the disciples as to which of them would be the greatest" (Lk 9:46).

It's as if he's speaking one language, and they're hearing another.

Even near the end of Jesus's ministry, when the journey to Jerusalem, and to death, is nearly complete, the disciples still expect to lead a kingdom of worldly power.

In Mark 10, James and John approach him privately with a request: "They said to him, 'Grant to us that we may sit, one at your right hand and one at your left hand, in your glory'" (Mk 10:37).

Jesus replies: "You don't know what you are asking. Are you able to drink the cup that I drink, and to be baptized with the baptism that I am baptized with?" (Mk 10:38)

It seems they believe he's on the verge of a worldly triumph, and they still can't see Jesus's true determination.

Even after Jesus's death and "resurrection," the misunderstanding lingers. We can see this confusion in Luke 24:21. On the road to Emmaus, two of Jesus's followers confess to a stranger, who turned out to be Jesus, that they had hoped Jesus would be the one to redeem Israel—to liberate them from Roman occupation.

So we can see that even three days after his crucifixion, they still expected a political deliverer, not understanding Jesus's true aim.

Again and again, the disciples, those closest to Jesus, failed to see what he was really doing.

This long arc of misunderstanding shows that those who walked with Jesus did not get it. And if they missed something so obvious, what else did they miss?

Chapter 12

The Satan

The story had ended, but something about the raising of Lazarus, which we witnessed in Chapter 7, kept tugging at my mind.

We've seen Jesus judge, break his own stated values, orchestrate his way to the cross, but I still couldn't understand *why*.

Then, I remembered what I learned while writing *The Genesis Code*, a book which focuses on Satan's role in the fall of humanity. In Hebrew, what we think of as the devil isn't Satan with a capital S. It's *the* satan, the accuser, the adversary, the prosecutor, the deceiver. A function, not a name. Like a legal title: the one who stands to oppose.

The answer was right there in the Book of Job. I had read it so many times, and even written about it, but for some reason, until this moment, I hadn't realized it also applied to Jesus.

I started thinking about all the religious leaders throughout history who spoke of God while sowing division. They are the ones who claim divine authority while serving themselves. They quote scripture with one breath and destroy with the next.

Why did this pattern keep repeating?

I pulled out my Bible, hunting for the Book of Job. There it is written that ha-satan walks freely in God's court, as a member of the divine council of angels. When God points out Job's righteousness, ha-satan responds:

"'Does Job fear God for nothing? Haven't you made a hedge around him, and around his house, and around all that he has, on every side? You have blessed the work of his hands, and his substance is increased in the land. But stretch out your hand now, and touch all that he has, and he will renounce you to your face'" (Jb 1:9–11).

He's suggesting that Job is untested, that he loves God only because his life has been blessed.

God gave Satan total power over all that Job had, while commanding him not to harm Job directly. Clearly God and ha-satan were working together, so I'm not sure it's fair to call ha-satan the enemy of God, at least within the context of the Book of Job.

In that story, Satan was God's prosecutor. He tested. He accused. He tore people down to see what they were made of.

In the Old Testament, Satan is conveyed as the voice of temptation, self-aggrandizement, condemnation and accusation, or anything that tests human faith in God. Ha-satan, in that context is the voice of sin, fundamentally.

Don't we all know that voice? I'd heard it so many times in my life: I'm not good enough. I'm better than them. I should be further along. At least I'm not like those people.

Back and forth. Self-condemnation and self-aggrandizement. The endless trial where I'm both prosecutor and defendant, trapped in judgment.

Isn't that the voice of ha-satan? It lives in every mind, does it not?

If this voice is in me, in you, in everyone, then maybe it was in Jesus, too. And if this voice lives in every human mind, what does that mean about God's relationship to the accuser?

I thought of how Genesis 1 showed God seeing only *good* in all creation. No polarizing judgment. No separation. Just endless recognition of its own nature in everything.

Scripture insists God is everywhere: "one God and Father of all, who is over all and through all and in us all" (Eph 4:6). "He is before all things, and in him all things are held together" (Col 1:17).

"... that God may be all in all" (1 Cor 15:28).

"where could I flee from your presence? If I ascend up into heaven, you are there. If I make my bed in Sheol, behold, you are there!" (Ps 139:7–8).

If God is truly *all*—not most, not some, but *all*—then what exactly would God be judging? Himself?

It seemed to me that if God judges anyone, then God is divided. That linked my mind to something Jesus said plainly: "Every kingdom divided against itself is brought to desolation, and every city or house divided against itself will not stand" (Mt 12:25).

If God judged, wouldn't that cause a division within God? What if that is what the fall from Eden was about? What if because Adam and Eve judged, they unconsciously divided themselves, falling into suffering and death?

Wouldn't that mean the undivided God does not judge?

This thought is backed by scripture: "For the Father judges no one, but he has given all judgment to the Son" (Jn 5:22).

I searched further and was stunned to find Jesus contradicting himself in the very same book. In John 8:15, he says, "You judge according to the flesh. I judge no one."

I was confused, and there doesn't seem to be any way to clear it up without straying too far from our exploration of Satan, so for now, let's return to the topic at hand. We'll return to the question of God's Judgment later.

Did you know the meaning and nature of Satan differs from the Old Testament to the New Testament? In the New Testament, Satan is not seen as a servant of God, but God's enemy, though that's never stated explicitly. It's a fundamental divide that accounts for much of the modern Christian views of Satan.

Wouldn't the belief that Satan is God's enemy lead us to hate and judge Satan? And aren't hate and judgment the voice of Satan?

It feels like we've been tricked, doesn't it?

Chapter 13

The Serpent

I flipped to Genesis 2 with a non-judging God in mind, and the story transformed before my eyes.

Two trees stood at the center of Eden. One tree offered eternal Life. The other offered suffering and death through judgment.

"Out of the ground Yahweh God made every tree to grow that is pleasant to the sight, and good for food, including the tree of life in the middle of the garden and the tree of the knowledge of good and evil" (Gn 2:9).

Then He took the man and put him into the garden of Eden to cultivate and keep it. Yahweh God commanded the man: "You may freely eat of every tree of the garden; but you shall not eat of the tree of the knowledge of good and evil; for in the day that you eat of it, you will surely die" (Gn 2:16-17).

Wait—what if this wasn't a threat, but a warning? Like saying don't touch the hot stove; you'll get burned? Don't judge; you'll suffer and die.

What if eating of the tree of judgment is to step out of Harmony and into separation, self-absorption, pride, shame and fear?

Then I arrived at Genesis 3, where the serpent approaches Eve with a seemingly innocent question: "Has God really said you can't eat from any tree in the garden?" (Gn 3:1)

Author's Note: while the Old Testament does not connect the serpent to Satan, the New Testament's Book of Revelation does in the following verses: Revelation 12:9: "The great dragon was hurled down—that ancient serpent called the devil, or Satan, who leads the whole world astray." Revelation 20:2: "He seized the dragon, that ancient serpent, who is the devil, or Satan, and bound him for a thousand years."

Returning to the question: notice the serpent's manipulation. He exaggerates the restriction, "you can't eat from any tree" to make God seem unreasonable. Eve corrects him, explaining they can eat from every tree except the one in the center.

Then comes the lie: "You won't really die. God knows that eating from it will open your eyes and make you like him—able to judge good and evil for yourselves" (Gn 3:4).

Isn't he suggesting that Adam and Eve can become the judge, independent from God?

Eve sees the fruit looks good, desires the wisdom it promises, and takes it. She gives some to Adam, who's standing right there. He eats too.

Their eyes open—but not to divine wisdom. They see themselves as naked and feel shame. For the first time, they experience judgment and separation. They hide from God's presence.

Then in Genesis 3:9 God calls out "Where are you?" This is odd. Wouldn't an omniscient God know where they were? Maybe this is like a father calling to children who are hiding, trying to draw them back into relationship.

But something has changed in Adam and Eve. They experience God's voice as threatening rather than loving because they know they have disobeyed God. A God who had to know they would do that. For Adam and Eve fear has taken over.

When God asks what happened, watch what unfolds: Adam blames Eve—and indirectly blames God himself. "The woman you gave me made me do it" (Gn 3:12). Eve blames the serpent. No one takes responsibility. Judgment has fractured their relationships with each other and with God.

Then comes the most shocking part of the story. The text records God cursing the serpent, condemning Eve to painful childbirth and male domination, and sentencing Adam to backbreaking labor until death. Finally, God drives them from Eden and posts armed cherubim to prevent their return, lest they also eat of the tree of life and gain immortality.

Wait. This is the same God who looked at all creation in Genesis 1 and saw that it was "very good"? The God who walked with them in the cool of the day? Something doesn't add up.

What if God didn't change—but Adam and Eve's perception of God changed? They've just eaten from the tree of judgment. Their consciousness has shifted into a polarizing, fear-based perspective.

In Genesis 3:10, Adam says, "I heard your voice in the garden, and I was afraid." What if that fear colored everything that followed?

The story reads as if God cursed and expelled them. But what if Adam and Eve, now seeing everything through the lens of judgment, could only experience God as a judge? What if they exiled themselves through shame, then projected that exile onto God?

What if when their eyes opened to judgment, everything looked like judgment, including God?

What if it was all ha-satan at work?

And what if from that moment forward, what we have called God has been nothing more than a reflection of our own fractured selves: a projection of fear, a bargaining with imagined wrath, a religion built on hallucination?

Maybe the mind that condemns estranges itself from the experience of God. And maybe that puts the mind at odds with God. Maybe ha-satan is the ego at war with its Source.

With scripture as our evidence, we can see that Jesus carried ha-satan, the accuser, just like we do. He judged the Pharisees as vipers. He sought glory for himself.

I closed my eyes and contemplated what I'd been discovering about Jesus. How he apparently sinned to engineer his crucifixion. How he'd let the satan speak through him.

If this was true—if ha-satan is the inner prosecutor, if God doesn't judge, if the fall from Eden was into judgment itself, then it means we have completely misunderstood the biblical narrative for thousands of years!

But there was another problem with the story. How could they understand the concept of death in a garden where nothing had ever died? They wouldn't be able to comprehend the consequences, would they?

It seems like a gaping hole in the Genesis story that I could not fill.

I shut down my computer and sat in the 3 a.m. darkness, deep in thought.

Chapter 14

The Christ

I woke up in a sweat. I missed something. My subconscious mind caught it. For hours I tossed and turned somewhere between this world and the next, my mind sifting and sorting, feeling for what I had overlooked.

All those breadcrumbs I'd been following—the deliberate sins, the orchestrated provocations, the staged performances—they were leading somewhere I never expected.

To understand this realization, we need to keep in mind how Satan's role evolved in Jewish theology. By Jesus's time, Jewish thought had transformed ha-satan from God's prosecutor into Satan—an independent adversary. The function had become a being opposed to God.

How did this shift occur?

The Old Testament presents ha-satan as God's prosecutor, but by Jesus's time, Jewish thought had transformed this into Satan as God's independent enemy.

As we saw in the last chapter, The New Testament explicitly records this connection in its final book, Revelation:

- o "The great dragon was hurled down—that ancient serpent called the devil, or Satan" (Rev 12:9).
- o "He seized the dragon, that ancient serpent, who is the devil, or Satan" (Rev 20:2).

Since Revelation was written after Jesus's death, it documents this theological shift without explaining how it occurred—only that it had become established Christian doctrine.

And that brings us back to Jesus. A disturbing pattern was emerging: *Every single thing that Satan would do to undermine Jesus's integrity, it seems Jesus was doing.*

No, I said out loud. No, that can't be. But the evidence was so compelling.

Every manipulation, every contradiction, every move—what if they weren't accidents? Think about it. Who delays while a friend dies to create a bigger spectacle? Who manipulates grief for personal glory? Who demands their followers disregard their families and even themselves?

My body shuddered as the possible implications dawned on me. The clues had been there from the very beginning.

At Cana, Jesus said no to his mother's request, but then performed the miracle anyway. The same power he refused to use for bread to save his own life, he used to make wine for a party.

He defied his own word—first to his mother at Cana, then to his brothers about the feast—despite teaching "Let your 'Yes' be 'Yes' and your 'No' be 'No.' Whatever is more than these is of the evil one."

He cursed a fig tree for not bearing fruit out of season: punishing it for following its own nature. Would a loving being do that?

The same glory he refused in the desert, he pursued through miraculous public performances.

Then when the Pharisees asked for a sign, he called them whitewashed tombs. Where was "love your enemies"? Where was "turn the other cheek"?

But perhaps the most glaring hypocrisy, a contradiction so blatant it is almost difficult to believe, is found in his own use of language. In the Sermon on the Mount, the very sermon where he commands unconditional love, Jesus sets the standard for speech:

"But I tell you that anyone who is angry with a brother or sister will be subject to judgment. Again, anyone who says to a brother or sister, 'Raca,' is answerable to the court. And anyone who says, 'You fool!' will be in danger of the fire of Gehenna" (Matthew 5:22).

The Greek word for "fool" here is *mōros*—from which we get our English word "moron." Jesus declares that using this single word against another is a sin worthy of hellfire.

Yet, in Matthew 23, during his public rant against the scribes and Pharisees, he shatters his own commandment with a stunning lack of self-awareness. He uses that exact word, *mōros*, repeatedly:

"Woe to you, blind guides! ... You blind fools!" (23:16-17)

"You fools and blind! For which is greater, the gift, or the altar that sanctifies the gift?" (23:17)

He called people fools just a few passages after warning that saying this to someone could land you in hell. Based on the exclamation marks in the text, he did it in anger, which is "subject to judgment."

The same blatant hypocrisy is seen with his statements about peacemakers in the Sermon on the Mount, when compared to what he says of his purpose just a few chapters later in Matthew:

In Matthew 5:9, he says, "Blessed are the peacemakers, for they will be called children of God." But just a few chapters later in Matthew 10:35-37, he says, "Do not suppose that I have come to bring peace to the earth. I did not come to bring peace, but a sword. For I have come to turn 'a man against his father, a daughter against her mother...'"

When Peter declared him the Messiah, essentially bowing in worship, Jesus immediately rewarded him with the keys of the kingdom. Is this the same transactional pattern we saw in the desert when Satan offered the keys to the kingdom if Jesus bowed to him?

At Lazarus's tomb, he staged his prayer so that onlookers would believe in and glorify him. What happened to "pray in your closet"?

And then there was his own explanation for why he taught in confusing parables. I can't believe I overlooked this.

When his disciples asked why he taught the masses in parables, Jesus gave a disturbing answer. He said he spoke in parables "because seeing they don't see, and hearing, they don't hear, neither do they understand," then quoted Isaiah:

"or else perhaps they might perceive with their eyes, hear with their ears, understand with their heart, and would turn again, and I would heal them" (Mt 13:14-15).

According to scripture, *he didn't want them to understand.* Otherwise, they might be healed. He was deliberately keeping people from understanding so they WOULDN'T be saved, so they wouldn't be free. Doesn't that mean he wanted them to suffer?

Even more disheartening, scripture explicitly says the truth was concealed from his disciples: "But they didn't understand this saying. It was concealed from them, that they should not perceive it, and they were afraid to ask him about this saying" (Lk 9:45).

Later: "Then he opened their minds, that they might understand the Scriptures" (Lk 24:45).

"He opened their minds": Which means what? That they had been kept shut? Remember the question in Chapter 11 about who concealed Jesus's aim to be crucified from the disciples? It seems we may have our answer.

Even the cross was performance: "My God, my God, why have you forsaken me?"—a word-for-word quote of Psalm 22:1.

It seems he played both sides. He became the victim of the scene he meticulously planned, and then he graciously forgave those he'd manipulated into executing him with "Father, forgive them, for they don't know what they are doing" (Lk 23:34).

When Jesus handed Judas the bread, the text says Satan entered into Judas. The text states explicitly that Satan entered Judas the moment he took the bread from Jesus. Who gave the bread? Who commanded Judas to act?

Am I implying that Jesus is Satan? I will direct you to what Jesus said about himself. You decide.

To Nicodemus, he compared himself to the bronze serpent Moses lifted in the wilderness: "As Moses lifted up the serpent in the wilderness, even so must the Son of Man be lifted up, that whoever believes in him should not perish, but have eternal life" (Jn 3:14-15).

The Christ

Jesus was referencing Numbers 21:6-9, where God told Moses to construct a bronze serpent on a pole for the Jews to look upon to be healed. This was the very image of what was killing the Israelites with snake bites.

But there is a deeper layer to this history that Jesus, as a Rabbi, surely knew. That bronze serpent didn't stay a tool of healing. It became a trap.

In 2 Kings 18:4, scripture records exactly what happened to that object: "He also broke in pieces the bronze serpent that Moses had made, because in those days the children of Israel burned incense to it; and he called it Nehushtan."

The Israelites had turned the healing tool into an idol. The name *Nehushtan* is often translated as **"The Great Serpent."**

Jesus would have known this history, as virtually every Jew of his time would have. Why would he connect himself to this story?

And, to my utter surprise, the Book of Revelation directly tells us who he is. He is called the "morning star." I looked that up—it means *Lucifer* in Latin: "I, Jesus, have sent my angel to testify these things to you for the assemblies. I am the root and the offspring of David, **the bright and morning star**" (Rev 22:16).

But there's more.

I shared these thoughts with a Christian friend, and he asked, "But don't the miracles prove Jesus is the Son of God?"

I remembered the story of Aaron battling the magicians in Egypt. It goes like this: "Aaron stretched out his hand over the waters of Egypt; and the frogs came up, and covered the land of Egypt. The magicians did the same thing with their enchantments, and brought up frogs on the land of Egypt" (Ex 8:6).

I researched the New Testament, and was stunned to find that Jesus explicitly warns about miracles in Matthew 24:24: *"For false messiahs and false prophets will appear and perform great signs and wonders to deceive, if possible, even the elect."* [emphasis mine]

What if he was talking about himself?

Even if I ignored all that evidence and agreed that Jesus is equal to God as the New Testament insists, the result was just as horrifying.

If God is all-knowing, as the Bible also insists, then he effectively engineered two thousand years of Jewish persecution. Countless millions dead. And he got away with it.

I had to stop writing. This was too disturbing.

__Author's Note:__ Some readers might question drawing conclusions from Revelation due to its apocalyptic literary style and symbolic language. However, this investigation examines the New Testament narrative as received, which is how the Fundamentalists and Literary Christians insist we read it. Therefore, this book treats Jesus's self-description as the morning star in Revelation 22:16 as part of the canonical narrative.

I discovered this connection simply by reading the texts. In Isaiah 14:12, the passage addresses an earthly king, then suddenly shifts to describing a being cast from heaven—"How you have fallen from heaven, morning star, son of the dawn!" When I encountered Revelation 22:16, where Jesus declares "I am... the bright and morning star," the connection was immediate.

Only afterward did I learn that Christianity had built centuries of theology around this same pattern. The original Hebrew "helel ben Shachar" (shining one, son of dawn) refers to the Babylonian king. In that account, the text describes a being who falls from heaven, using the title "morning star." When Jerome translated this into Latin in the 4th century as "Lucifer" (light-bearer), Christian theology gradually transformed it into a proper name for Satan. By medieval times, "Lucifer = Satan = the fallen morning star" was established doctrine.

This created an unavoidable problem. Whether you read it in Hebrew (Helel), Latin (Lucifer), or English (Morning Star), Jesus uses the exact title that Isaiah used to describe the being who fell from heaven for wanting to be like the Most High. I did not need theology to see this connection—the texts present it plainly when read straightforwardly. Christian doctrine simply confirmed what was already there in the narrative.

Why Christianity would develop and maintain theology that equates Jesus with Lucifer remains unclear. Whether this was unintentional blindness, deliberate warning, or something else entirely, the connection exists in the texts they canonized and the interpretations they established.

Chapter 15

Hidden in Plain Sight

I retired for the night and returned to it the next morning, realizing I needed to investigate Christian teachings, rituals, and structures to see whether they support or undermine the Satan hypothesis.

I remembered the core Christian message: Jesus will save us from God's wrath, *if we accept him into our hearts.* Think about that. Save us—from God.

Where does the shame come from that makes us need saving? *You are sinners, wretches; You'll go to Hell unless you accept Jesus.*

Manipulative marketing 101: First create the problem. Then offer the solution.

When I started looking at the practices objectively, I was stunned to see the following as well: asking spirits to possess you (being filled with the holy spirit), ritually consuming symbolic flesh and blood, practicing ritual drowning and resurrection (baptism), allowing entities to speak through you (speaking in tongues), and wearing execution devices as holy symbols.

The list goes on.

I sat staring at this evidence, aghast. I had never thought of these practices in this dark light before, but after realizing that the Book of Revelation claims the title of the Morning Star for Jesus, and considering he infected Judas with Satan, this dark lens seems appropriate.

You must admit, they would appear to be very suspicious practices to anyone not within the fold. Especially if they knew Jesus identified with the same title as the fallen celestial being in Isaiah's taunt to the king of Babylon.

If this pattern is real, we'd expect there to be compelling evidence beyond scripture. There is, and it is remarkably easy to find.

The architecture commonly reflects what you might expect from Satan: gothic cathedrals adorned with gargoyles—demons carved into holy buildings—fit the theme precisely.

Then there is the hall where the Pope gives audiences. It's designed to look just like a serpent's head (eyes, fangs, and scales). Inside the mouth of the serpent is a bronze sculpture by Fazzini that appears to depict either Jesus or Satan rising from flames, depending on the angle from which it is viewed. It's an extremely disturbing image, especially given that it is found within the mouth of the serpent.

Coincidence?

If someone had merely told me these things, I would have assumed it was a ridiculous conspiracy theory. A building shaped like a snake? A demonic-looking Jesus rising from flames in the mouth of a serpent? It sounds impossible.

I cannot legally print the images here due to copyright restrictions, so I am asking you to stop reading for a moment. Pick up your phone. Search for **"Paul VI Audience Hall interior snake"** and **"La Resurrezione Fazzini statue."**

Look at the eyes (the oval windows). Look at the fangs (the supporting pillars). Look at the scales (the roof and walls). These aren't hidden secrets; they are publicly visible architectural choices. Once you see them with your own eyes, you cannot unsee them.

There is also the pastoral staff carried by bishops in both Eastern Orthodox and Roman Catholic traditions. These staves sometimes feature two serpents or dragons facing each other, with a cross between them. These traditions claim it represents the bronze serpent Moses erected in the wilderness. Jesus, who claimed the Morning Star title associated with the fallen celestial being, compared himself to the serpent being lifted up.

Was he following an ancient occult principle that requires deceptive entities to signal their true nature and obtain consent, even if cryptically? The logic behind this principle is not about fairness; it's about shifting responsibility.

By providing the warning (however hidden) and gaining consent (however manipulated), the entity can claim that the victim was not truly deceived, but that they *chose* their own fate. It transforms an act of deception into a voluntary contract.

The occult imagery could serve as both warning and disclosure, while practices like "inviting Jesus into your heart" provide the consent mechanism. Those who see the symbols but choose to participate have technically been informed.

Why has the Christian community largely overlooked all this evidence?

Two billion people following these practices, all of it flowing from one source. We don't seem to realize it.

I couldn't finish the thought. My whole body was sweating.

This was not at all where I thought my promise to Jesus would lead. But the evidence was overwhelming.

I retired to another night of restless sleep.

Chapter 16

King of Kings

I woke up early the next morning, about 3:30 AM, thinking about Jesus. I was too restless to return to sleep, so I rose and began my research afresh with Matthew, searching for anything I might have missed.

At the end of Matthew, Jesus declares his ultimate claim: "Jesus came to them and spoke to them, saying, 'All authority has been given to me in heaven and on earth. Go, and make disciples of all nations, baptizing them in the name of the Father and of the Son and of the Holy Spirit, teaching them to observe all things that I commanded you. Behold, I am with you always, even to the end of the age.' Amen" (Mt 28:18-20).

Though I had read that passage many times in the past, this time it took on a whole new meaning.

"All authority in heaven and on earth has been given to me." That's not just claiming to be a king or even the Messiah. Only someone equal to God would have ALL authority in heaven AND earth, right?

What does Jesus use that power for? Glory. Global worship. Obedience. John 12:32 shows the intention: "And I, if I am lifted up from the earth, will draw all people to myself." Not to God. Not to truth. *To himself.*

Have we been looking at the very serpent that has been poisoning us for thousands of years, mistaking it for our salvation?

Then I remembered the Christian lore on Lucifer: Lucifer, the light bearer, was God's first angel. The first and most beloved Son of God who, due to his prideful Ego, fell from heaven for wanting to be equal to God.

We can see that sentiment in Paul's letter to the Philippians: "...that at the name of Jesus every knee should bow, in heaven and on earth and under the earth, and every tongue acknowledge that Jesus Christ is Lord..." (Phil 2:10-11).

There it was. Not a request, but a demand for total, universal submission. Maybe the King of Kings, that wise old serpent, had fooled us all.

My mind returned to Jesus gaining all power in heaven and earth. Wouldn't that mean Jesus had risen to the throne in Eden?

I flipped to the back of my Bible and found a description of the grand event.

The Book of Revelation explains: "He showed me a river of water of life, clear as crystal, proceeding out of the throne of God and of the Lamb, in the middle of its street. On this side of the river and on that was the tree of life, bearing twelve kinds of fruits, yielding its fruit every month. The leaves of the tree were for the healing of the nations. There will be no curse anymore. The throne of God and of the Lamb will be in it, and his servants will serve him" (Rev 22:1-3).

The Lamb? The "Lamb" title connects to John the Baptist's declaration in John 1:29: "Behold, the Lamb of God, who takes away the sin of the world!" That's Jesus. The Lamb was *on* the throne, sharing power with God, just as Lucifer claimed *he* would.

Then I read the passage again and noticed something I had missed during the first readthrough. It said, "there will be no curse anymore." I had to refresh my memory of the specifics of the curse. I found it in Genesis, right after Adam and Eve ate from the forbidden tree.

God cursed them with pain in childbirth, backbreaking labor, and death itself: "In pain you will bear children... cursed is the ground for your sake. In toil you will eat of it all the days of your life... By the sweat of your face will you eat bread until you return to the ground, for you are dust, and you shall return to dust" (Gn 3:16-19).

Pain in childbirth, struggling to grow food, death itself—these were the curses. But Revelation claims these curses will be gone. If Jesus truly took the throne and lifted the curse, then we should no longer experience these things, right?

Has he not already taken the throne? The end of Matthew claims he was granted all authority in heaven and on earth. Shouldn't all Christians be immortal now? Why do they still get sick like anyone else?

Chapter 17

The Light-Bearer

After completing my analysis of Jesus, I had a feeling that something was not quite right in my theory. I thought Jesus was Satan. But, after a few days, I knew this conclusion had to be false.

I searched Bible Gateway, and I found scriptural evidence exonerating Jesus. Remember the scene in the desert where Jesus is tempted by Satan. How could Jesus have been tempted by Satan if he was Satan?

What about possession? Maybe the desert scene was Jesus talking to Satan in his head, the one that had been trying to possess him.

Remember the parable of the sower? Jesus said: "The ones by the road are the ones where the word is sown; and when they have heard, immediately Satan comes and takes away the word which has been sown in them" (Mk 4:15).

It's another statement proving Jesus could NOT be Satan. But this passage also suggests he was not possessed by Satan. If he were possessed by Satan, why would he warn about Satan derailing believers?

That got me thinking. Jesus is identified as the "morning star," which means Lucifer in Latin. I had always assumed, as Christian lore teaches, that Satan and Lucifer were synonymous. What if they aren't? I had a lot of research ahead of me.

I went back to the Book of Job, where I'd first encountered the term ha-satan. I read it with fresh eyes. It goes like this: "Now on the day when God's sons came to present themselves before Yahweh, Satan also came among them. Yahweh said to Satan, 'Where have you come from?' Then Satan answered Yahweh, and said, 'From going back and forth in the earth, and from walking up and down in it'" (Jb 1:6–7).

The relationship was clear: Satan reports TO the Lord God like a servant reports to his master. Satan is the prosecutor, the tester, the accuser who serves a higher power.

So, we know who Satan is and who he served in Eden. Who is Lucifer?

My research for the origin of the "Lucifer" character led me to the book of Isaiah, and to a passage of remarkable complexity. To understand it, we must first see its structure. The text presents a four-layered communication:

1. **The Source:** Yahweh (The Lord of Armies) originates the message.
2. **The Prophet:** The message is given to the prophet Isaiah.
3. **The Speakers:** Isaiah instructs the nation of Israel to be the ones who will speak the message.
4. **The Subject:** The message itself is a "parable" or taunt song to be directed *at* the king of Babylon.

Within this structure, the prophet instructs the people of Israel to deliver the following taunt **against** their fallen oppressor. **I** will present the relevant text, so you can see the context. Bracketed comments are my clarifications.

Isaiah 14:4, 9-10, 12-16, 22-23:

> *You [the nation of Israel] will take up this parable against the king of Babylon, and say, 'How the oppressor has ceased! The golden city has ceased!' ...*
>
> *Sheol from beneath is excited about you to meet you at your coming. It stirs up the dead for you... It has raised up from their thrones all the kings of the nations. They all will answer and ask you, "Have you also become as weak as we are? Have you become like us?" ...*
>
> *How you have fallen from heaven, shining one, son of the dawn! How you are cut down to the ground, who laid the nations low!*
>
> *You said in your heart, "I will ascend into heaven! I will exalt my throne above the stars of God! I will sit on the mountain of assembly, in the far north! I will ascend above the heights of the clouds! I will make myself like the Most High!"*

Yet you shall be brought down to Sheol, to the depths of the pit. Those who see you will stare at you. They will ponder you, saying, "Is this the man who made the earth to tremble, who shook kingdoms ...?"

[Then the voice shifts to Yahweh speaking directly]

"I will rise up against them," says Yahweh of Armies, "and cut off from Babylon name and remnant, and son and son's son," says Yahweh. "I will also make it a possession for the porcupine, and pools of water. I will sweep it with the broom of destruction," says Yahweh of Armies.

I have skipped over aspects of the taunt that are not relevant to our exploration here, but feel free to read the full text in your Bible or on biblegateway.com

Reading this full context of the relevant text, the dual nature of the passage is undeniable.

It begins as a message for the king of Babylon, a human tyrant. But in the middle of this, the text seems to pivot to describe a being whose ambition was cosmic: a "shining one" who has "fallen from heaven" and whose goal, in his own words, was to be "like the Most High."

The passage itself intertwines the two figures, using the story of the fallen celestial being to mock the arrogance of the fallen king. It is this description of the "shining one, son of the dawn"—*Helel ben Shachar* in Hebrew, translated as *Lucifer* in Latin—that provides the biblical character and ambitions of the ultimate Ego.

And the connection was immediate when I remembered the words of Jesus in Revelation, where he claims that very same title for himself: **"I, Jesus... am the root and the offspring of David, the bright and morning star"** (Rev 22:16).

The text, as we have received it, makes a direct link. Our investigation is based on this textual evidence. We are simply following what is written on the page.

A note on translations: The Hebrew word "helel" *in Isaiah 14:12 is translated differently across Bible versions. The KJV uses "Lucifer," the NIV uses "morning star," and the WEB uses "shining one" and "son of the dawn"—but all refer to the same fallen figure, the light-bearer being who fell from heaven.*

This is the same title Jesus claims in Revelation 22:16: "the bright and morning star." The fact that translators consistently avoid using "Lucifer" in Revelation

22:16, despite Jesus claiming the same title that Isaiah 14:12 associates with the fallen figure, could be seen as apologetic translation choices that mask the similarity.

You might be thinking, "Wait. The text clearly states Yahweh (YHWH) was addressing the king of Babylon, not talking to Lucifer."

Yes, but here is the real point. Regardless of who he was talking to, Yahweh both names and describes the character and ambitions of the "morning star," or Lucifer in the Latin translation, in the process of berating the king.

Our investigation is based on the direct textual evidence that Jesus, in the book of Revelation, calls himself by this very same title: "I am... the bright and morning star." *The text provides the direct link: Jesus claims the exact title that the Old Testament associates with the fallen aspirant to God's throne. Within the narrative of the Bible, the connection is explicit.*

A biblically knowledgeable reader might make a grammatical argument, suggesting that in Isaiah, "morning star" is a proper noun (a name), while in Revelation, it is merely a descriptive adjective (a title). But even if we grant this distinction, it does not solve the problem.

It would mean that Jesus is knowingly and deliberately choosing to identify himself with a title that is explicitly associated in his own scripture with the ultimate symbol of cosmic pride and rebellion. Why choose this toxic, compromised title?

This brings us back to the ancient occult principle we discussed earlier: the idea that a deceptive entity must, in some way, signal its true nature. By making this direct, undeniable, yet grammatically ambiguous connection, the character of Jesus provides the perfect "cosmic fine print." For a believer, he is simply a "bright star." But what if he was providing a warning? Maybe he has signaled his identity, in a masterful act of plausible deniability.

The following is just my speculation on the topic and could be wrong.

I wondered if the text was describing a case of spiritual possession. If the King of Babylon was possessed by this "Morning Star" entity, it would explain the odd, sudden shift in Isaiah from addressing a human king to addressing a heavenly being. Let me lay out the theory for your exploration. It explains a lot that current Christian thinking does not.

Though it doesn't matter if Yahweh was addressing the king of Babylon, Lucifer or both simultaneously, the description of the dark voice is there. Just like Jesus, the king of Babylon claimed to be equal to God.

Let's explore the idea that Yahweh was speaking to both the king and Lucifer. Imagine the king was possessed by Lucifer. Wouldn't that explain the odd, sudden shift from addressing a human king to addressing a heavenly being.

The narcissism shown by Jesus and described in the king of Babylon is identical, as are their aspirations of being equal to God. If Jesus and the king of Babylon were possessed by Lucifer at different times, their God claims and shared characteristics make perfect sense.

In any case, from direct textual evidence we can see this Cosmic Ego, Lucifer, wanted to be worshipped like God. *What if he succeeded?*

Author's Note: *The thought of Jesus possibly being possessed by Lucifer was personally quite disturbing. After a long pause I realized that I, like many people, have a deeply rooted negative bias against the name Lucifer. Through Christian lore and popular culture, we have been conditioned to associate it with the ultimate evil, the adversary of all that is good. That conditioning makes it almost impossible to see this connection objectively.*

As an investigator, I had to set aside the emotional weight of the name and look strictly at the pattern—the demand for worship, the desire for glory, the punishment of rivals. The behavior is identical. The text links them by title, but I believe it's more important to see the behavior.

Moving forward, we will continue to explore biblical evidence linking Jesus and Lucifer, but please be mindful to separate the biblical Lucifer from the associations we have inherited through pop culture.

As an aside, did you notice that Yahweh (YHWH) self-described as "Yahweh of Armies"? Does that sound like a loving God? We'll be revisiting this point later in the book. You might keep it in mind.

Chapter 18

The Messianic Relationship

Let's imagine the scenario, where Jesus is Lucifer's vessel to see where it takes us. If Jesus really was Lucifer's vessel, then the biblical text should show evidence of this relationship. It was surprisingly easy to find.

The Gospel of Luke records: "Now there was a man in Jerusalem called Simeon, who was righteous and devout. He was waiting for the consolation of Israel, and the Holy Spirit was on him. It had been revealed to him by the Holy Spirit that he would not die before he had seen the Lord's Messiah" (Lk 2:25-27).

The possessive was unmistakable. Not just the Messiah, but the *Lord's* Messiah. It creates the impression that the Messiah belongs to and serves the Lord, doesn't it? That would make sense, because *Messiah* means the one anointed to serve God.

Even more telling was something Jesus himself said in Mark 13:19-20: "for they will be days of oppression, such as has not been from the beginning of the creation which God created until now, and never will be. Unless the Lord had shortened the days, no flesh would have been saved; but for the sake of the chosen ones, whom he picked out, he shortened the days."

This saying is similarly recorded in Matthew 24:21-22: "for then there will be great oppression, such as has not been from the beginning of the world until now, no, nor ever will be. Unless those days had been shortened, no flesh would have been saved. But for the sake of the chosen ones, those days will be shortened."

Why would Jesus speak of the Lord in third person as if the Lord is someone else entirely? And he speaks of the Lord as if he is the ultimate decision-maker. This passage creates the impression that Jesus is not claiming to be the Lord himself but rather reporting on what the Lord will do.

What if the Lord is Lucifer? That would mean Jesus is Lucifer's Messiah—his chosen vessel—not God's. The thought was unsettling, but the pattern seemed to be a perfect fit.

It was late, and I was exhausted, so I retired for the evening. I woke up early the next morning from a dream, and in it I saw the Spirit descend upon Jesus like a dove at his baptism. As I watched, I remembered Paul's warning in his epistles: "No wonder, for even Satan masquerades as an angel of light" (2 Corinthians 11:14). Then, everything clicked.

If Satan could do this, couldn't his superior, Lucifer, do this?

What if the Spirit that descended like a dove (Matthew 3:17) and declared that Jesus is his beloved Son, in whom he is well pleased wasn't YHWH blessing Jesus, but the imposter claiming his chosen vessel?

I sat up in bed, fully awake. If Lucifer had been masquerading as "the Lord" since Genesis 3:8, then the revered baptism scene might be the moment of ultimate deception, witnessed by John the Baptist and accepted as holy by everyone present.

It was a radical thought that means nothing without biblical evidence to back it. I returned to my Bible.

You know the Transfiguration from Matthew 17? It's when Jesus changed before his disciples, his face shining like the sun, his garments as white as the light. For two thousand years, Christianity has pointed to this as proof of Jesus's virtue.

But considering Paul's warning that Satan masquerades as an angel of light, could this scene be revealing something else? When his face shone "like the sun" and his clothes became "white as light," was this a revelation of divinity, or the unveiling of the Light-Bearer?

This brought my attention to John the Baptist, at the place in the text where his disciples were arguing about who could give baptism.

When John's disciples become concerned about Jesus's growing following, they complain to John that the man he testified about was baptizing, and everyone was going to him instead of John.

John's response was a sweeping endorsement that essentially declared Jesus to be divine. He said Jesus came from heaven while earthly people belonged to earth. He claimed Jesus spoke God's words and had God's Spirit without limit. Most remarkably, he declared that "the Father loves the Son, and has given all things into his hand" (Jn 3:35).

Then came the ultimate threat: "One who believes in the Son has eternal life, but one who disobeys the Son won't see life, but the wrath of God remains on him" (Jn 3:25–36).

John essentially declared Jesus as the Messiah and possibly even the Lord God himself.

If Lucifer had been masquerading as "the Lord" since Genesis 3:8, then what about John, who served that same "Lord"? Was John deceived into believing he served the true God, or was he knowingly complicit in preparing the way for Lucifer?

Jesus doesn't leave any ambiguity about John's endorsement. When the Samaritan woman mentioned the coming Messiah, Jesus declared plainly: "I am he who speaks to you" (Jn 4:26).

If this theory is correct, it reframes Jesus's statement entirely. Was he speaking honestly here, admitting that he was the anointed servant of a different Lord?

The relationship between John the Baptist, Jesus, and "the Lord" is clear: divine endorsement from the most recognized prophet of that time, followed by explicit self-declaration from Jesus.

Both John and Jesus serve the same Lord—and if that Lord is Lucifer, then that changes everything we think we know about the Gospels and Christianity.

But did they know who "the Lord" really was? I can't find any evidence one way or the other.

If Lucifer had been masquerading as YHWH throughout Jesus's ministry, then the entire baptism sequence takes on a new flavor.

The same Spirit that claimed Jesus as "my beloved Son" at the baptism immediately led him into the wilderness to be tempted by Satan. If this theory is correct, it wasn't God testing Jesus, but Lucifer using Satan to test his servant, ensuring his chosen vessel would be completely obedient to his will.

What if the desert test was Lucifer's final vetting process? Let's imagine it.

He needed to confirm that Jesus would follow orders without question, even under extreme duress. When Jesus passed every test by refusing to act independently, Lucifer knew he had found the perfect servant—someone who would follow the script exactly, even unto death.

Scripture itself demonstrates that others were suspicious: "The scribes who came down from Jerusalem said, 'He has Beelzebul,' and, 'By the prince of the demons, he casts out demons'" (Mk 3:22).

Beelzebul was another name for Satan. So they were directly accusing Jesus of being possessed by the devil himself.

Jesus did not deny it.

Instead, he responded: "How can Satan cast out Satan? If a kingdom is divided against itself, that kingdom cannot stand. If a house is divided against itself, that house cannot stand. If Satan has risen up against himself, and is divided, he can't stand, but has an end" (Mk 3:23-26).

But Jesus's house DID fall.

He was crucified, and fell into the heart of the earth, according to his own words in Matthew 12:40: "For as Jonah was three days and three nights in the belly of a huge fish, so the Son of Man will be three days and three nights in the heart of the earth."

Even if Jesus rose to heaven after the third day, Christianity teaches that he fell into hell first.

Maybe casting out demons and judging others was how he weakened himself, so he could be crucified. Do you remember his teaching about reaping what you sow? Unless you are perfect, you will be cast in the fire. Those are Jesus's ideas.

When the chief priests and teachers of the law questioned his authority, he deflected: "I will ask you one question. Answer me, and I will tell you by what

90

authority I do these things. The baptism of John—was it from heaven, or from men? Answer me" (Mk 11:29–30).

When they refused to answer, Jesus said, "Neither will I tell you by what authority I do these things" (Mk 11:33).

Jesus's behavior seemed very suspicious. He was putting tremendous effort into hiding his identity and the source of his power.

As I sat there reviewing my notes, I realized the scope of the apparent deception was beyond anything I could have anticipated.

Then I found something that seemed to bolster my theory even further. Luke 12:8: "I tell you, whoever confesses me before men, the Son of Man will also confess before the angels of God."

It reads to me like a cosmic transaction: "Acknowledge me before others, and I'll acknowledge you."

Isn't that exactly what the Lord of Narcissism would say?

And that got me wondering. What would it be like to serve Lord Lucifer? Imagine the stereotypical, egotistically driven boss.

Now, let's see what Jesus said about the ideal relationship with the Lord: "But who is there among you, having a servant plowing or keeping sheep, that will say when he comes in from the field, 'Come immediately and sit down at the table'? Wouldn't he rather say to him, 'Prepare my supper, clothe yourself properly, and serve me while I eat and drink. Afterward you shall eat and drink'? Does he thank that servant because he did the things that were commanded? I think not. Even so you also, when you have done all the things that are commanded you, say, 'We are unworthy servants. We have done our duty'" (Lk 17:7–10).

Work all day, come home and serve more, expect no thanks. Afterwards, you can eat, but be sure to call yourself "unworthy."

Unworthy?

Isn't this a judgment of self-worth? Doesn't "I am unworthy" feel like pure self-condemnation? Isn't Jesus violating his own teaching: Judge not?

It seems to me like the perfect system for narcissistic supply: devoted servants who work tirelessly while being programmed to be grateful just to serve.

In any system of master and servant, there is an ultimate enforcement mechanism. If we are "unworthy," who decides our fate?

This raised another disturbing question about the day of judgment. If Jesus was Lucifer's vessel, and Christians were unknowingly serving a Cosmic Ego, what did that mean for the Day of Judgment that so many feared? Who would really oversee this ultimate evaluation of souls?

The answers Jesus provides regarding this question are puzzling: "I have come as a light into the world, that whoever believes in me should not remain in the darkness. If anyone listens to my sayings and doesn't believe, *I don't judge him. For I came not to judge the world, but to save the world*" (Jn 12:46-47). [emphasis mine]

Yet earlier, he had said: "For the Father judges no one, but he has given all judgment to the Son" (Jn 5:22).

And again: "He also gave him authority to execute judgment, because he is a son of man" (Jn 5:27).

You might remember my confusion in Chapter 12, when wondering whether God judged or not. Still, I can find no answer to this vital question.

These seem like contradictory claims about something fundamental. What do we make of testimony that can't stay consistent on such basic questions?

Chapter 19

The System

We've seen Jesus linked to the morning star in the Book of Revelation. We have seen the shared character and aim they expressed. And we have seen the case for Jesus being Lucifer's Messiah.

Now, let's look at Jesus's recruitment system, to see what evidence may be there.

Before examining how this system operates, it's important to understand Lucifer's motivations based on biblical text, not on the ideas of Lucifer found in pop culture.

Continuing with the theory that Jesus was Lucifer's vessel, let's map out what Lucifer's motivations might be based on what Jesus desired.

According to evidence in the Gospels, he doesn't want humanity to suffer for suffering's sake, which is to say, he isn't evil in the sense we typically imagine. Based on Jesus's statements and the description of Lucifer's desire in Isaiah, we can see that he craves attention, recognition, and worship. He wants to be loved and adored as God.

This might explain why the system as described above emphasizes love, service, and community—not because he cares about "goodness," but because these qualities create the most effective recruitment and retention strategy.

Virtue and generosity attract more converts. Fellowship keeps people engaged. Love generates genuine devotion rather than mere fear-based compliance.

It's sophisticated spiritual marketing: create sustainable religious communities that produce maximum worship while genuinely caring for their members. The "goodness" serves the ultimate goal—extracting as much adoration as possible from as many people as possible.

With this understanding, let's examine how the system works.

Do you remember our discussion about the Jewish laws regarding consuming blood? It's forbidden because to the Jews the blood contained the life or spirit of the creature. The Jewish kosher law wasn't just about physical health but about spiritual purity and maintaining proper boundaries between different forms of life/spirit.

But didn't Jesus command exactly what Jewish law forbade? He said: "Most certainly I tell you, unless you eat the flesh of the Son of Man and drink his blood, you don't have life in yourselves" (Jn 6:53).

To give you a sense of the tradition that developed from this statement, let's consider the Eucharist. In the Catholic and Orthodox traditions, for example, the bread and wine are thought to literally transform into Christ's actual body and blood (it's called transubstantiation), though they retain the appearance of bread and wine.

Maybe this was the mechanism: symbolic consumption of Jesus's blood/flesh through communion, faith as the requisite psychological opening, desire to be filled by the Holy Spirit as explicit invitation. The result? Spirit possession by Lucifer masquerading as the Holy Spirit.

What if Christians were unknowingly inviting his consciousness into their hearts through faith-enabled ritual consumption? It's a disturbing thought, but that was only a part of the mechanism, I suspected.

Jesus is asking for entry. "He who eats my flesh and drinks my blood lives in me, and I in him" (John 6:56).

"I in him." It's a specific, internal phrasing.

I looked to Paul to see how this mechanism played out in practice. Paul, the model convert, describes the result of this process with total clarity in Galatians 2:20: "It is no longer I who live, but Christ lives in me."

I read that line again. *It is no longer I who live.*

If the "I"—the individual self—is no longer living, and Christ is living through that body instead, isn't that a displacement?

If Jesus is indeed the Cosmic Ego we identified in previous chapters—the entity that craves total glory and attention—then this mechanism makes perfect sense. He doesn't just want to be worshipped from the outside; he wants to be the only one acting, the only one living, through millions of bodies.

It raises a difficult question about integrity: Does a being of true integrity want to replace you? Or would they want you to become fully, authentically yourself?

To understand why anyone would accept such a bargain, I looked at his other threat.

While researching, I noticed how different Jesus's tone was from the wrathful deity of much of the Old Testament. The loving teachings, the sacrifice, the *I died for you* message that he is cherished for. But we must not forget the lake of fire.

The wrathful Old Testament deity threatened death, exile, destruction—finite punishments. The eternal punishments he offered were shame and everlasting contempt. It was Jesus who brought us the concept of infinite torture. Look at the actual threats:

Jesus said this of God: "Then he will say also to them on the left hand, 'Depart from me, you cursed, into the eternal fire which is prepared for the devil and his angels!' These will go away into eternal punishment, but the righteous into eternal life" (Mt 25:41, 46).

This represents a marked escalation from the Jewish idea of eternal shame and condemnation detailed in Daniel 12:2: "Many of those who sleep in the dust of the earth will awake, some to everlasting life, and some to shame and everlasting contempt" (Dan 12:2). So, it seems, Jesus didn't replace fear with love. He perfected fear by combining it with love.

Think about the psychological brilliance of this approach: Jesus creates the ultimate terror (eternal torture), then offers himself as the rescue. The same entity threatening infinite punishment graciously provides the escape route.

Now humans aren't just afraid; they're grateful. *He loves me so much he died to save me—from the hell he created.*

Matthew 25:40 tells us who gets saved from this eternal torture: "those who take care of the least of these my brethren"—Jesus's followers, and those who take care of his followers. Not humanity as a whole.

Doesn't that sound a lot like a protection racket?

Take care of my people, and I'll take care of you. Ignore them, and I'll have you tortured forever.

But for some reason, we tend to overlook that he introduced the ultimate threat and then offered a golden bridge for our escape, which is that we believe in and obey him.

Which would generate more devoted worship, fear or love? The real answer is *both*, it seems.

Those who joined didn't just submit to Jesus; they also loved him, because in their minds, he saved their souls from the eternal fire of hell, from God's wrathful judgment.

I could see this as Jesus making himself appear merciful at God's expense: Love Jesus; Fear God.

Because of this strategy, Christians worship with genuine affection rather than mere fearful obedience, as was the case prior to Jesus.

The most famous verse in Christianity perfectly demonstrates this psychological fusion; John 3:16: "For God so loved the world, that he gave his only born Son, that whoever believes in him should not perish, but have eternal life."

See also John 3:18: "One who believes in him is not judged. He who doesn't believe has been judged already, because he has not believed in the name of the only born Son of God."

And John 3:36 continues the theme: "One who believes in the Son has eternal life, but one who disobeys the Son won't see life, but the wrath of God remains on him."

Do you see it? In a single breath, the threat is woven into the love. You literally cannot quote the love without the condemnation being right there in the context.

With eternal torment on the line, it's vital that we know what could damn us. According to Jesus there is only one unforgiveable sin, blasphemy against the Holy Spirit.

To avoid crossing that critical line, we need to know who or what the Holy Spirit is. Have you ever seen it defined clearly in the Bible?

We know that the Father is God. We know that God is the creator. We know the Son is Jesus (or possibly Lucifer). But who or what is the Holy Spirit? Where is it defined?

The Old Testament mentions *ruach hakodesh*—holy wind, breath, or spirit—but it's vague. Sometimes it seems to be God's presence, sometimes divine inspiration, sometimes just God's power in action.

The New Testament isn't much clearer. Sometimes the Holy Spirit appears to be God's presence at Pentecost; sometimes it's described as "another Comforter" like Jesus, sometimes it's treated as a person who can be grieved or lied to, and sometimes it's just divine power or wisdom.

Yet according to Jesus, there is only one unforgivable sin: blaspheming against the Holy Spirit. "Therefore I tell you, every sin and blasphemy will be forgiven people, but the blasphemy against the Spirit will not be forgiven" (Matthew 12:31).

But what does blasphemy even mean?

Traditionally, it means speaking irreverently or disrespectfully about God or sacred things. In the context where Jesus makes this statement, the Pharisees had accused him of casting out demons by Satan's power rather than God's power. Jesus labels this accusation—attributing God's work to Satan—as blasphemy against the Holy Spirit.

Here's the problem: if we don't know what the Holy Spirit is, how can we possibly know what constitutes speaking irreverently about it? How can someone avoid committing an eternal offense against something that's never clearly defined?

The vagueness creates the perfect theological wildcard. Is questioning Jesus's harsh judgments blasphemy against the Spirit? What about pointing out contradictions in scripture? Is it damning to suggest that threatening people with eternal torture doesn't seem loving? Without clear boundaries, any criticism of religious authority could potentially be labeled blasphemous.

It seems like the ultimate gaslighting: define the only unforgivable crime as something invisible, so the person is always afraid they might have accidentally committed it.

This moral system makes the very act of honest inquiry spiritually dangerous, because the rules about what constitutes "irreverence" are unclear. The undefined Holy Spirit becomes the ultimate enforcement mechanism: threatening enough to silence criticism through fear of eternal consequences, yet vague enough to be applied to any inconvenient questioning.

Consider a question that is logically necessary, yet spiritually dangerous to ask: According to Jesus, he already watched Satan's fall from Heaven. Jesus already rose to the throne in Eden. He's already in the Judge's seat. Why hasn't the curse been removed even for believers?

If believers question if Satan already fell, then they may be blaspheming against Jesus. The fact that Christians still suffer and die—what does that imply?

It seems to me that whoever is not already in heaven on earth (immortal), must have committed the unforgiveable sin. Surely that can't be true of everyone. What about babies, who can't yet speak?

By making salvation criteria unknowable and making questioning itself potentially damning, this set of beliefs ensures compliance through fear rather than genuine understanding. Aside from the Sermon on the Mount, which we will discuss later, we can see these traps all through scripture.

I could see how fear-traps help keep members in the fold, but what I didn't fully understand was the recruitment system. What makes people want to become Christian?

I reviewed Mark 4 and found something that seemed to explain recruitment. Jesus describes different types of people like soil types: Some hear the message, but Satan immediately takes it away. Others receive it joyfully but fall away when persecution comes. Still others get choked out by worldly concerns and wealth.

But the "good soil" people? They bear fruit at different rates—thirty, sixty, or even one hundred times what was planted.

Then comes the revealing part: "For whoever has, to him more will be given; and he who doesn't have, even that which he has will be taken away from him" (Mk 4:25).

The hierarchy was explicit: those who successfully convert followers get promoted, while those who fail lose standing.

And the reward structure? In Mark 4:30, Jesus promised that anyone who left family and possessions for his sake would "receive one hundred times more now in this time: houses, brothers, sisters, mothers, children, and land, with persecutions; and in the age to come eternal life."

It read to me like a complete business model: personality profiling (soil types), conversion metrics (30x, 60x, 100x returns), performance hierarchy, and concrete material incentives.

One could argue that Christianity's aggressive evangelical mandate resembles a spiritual pyramid structure with Lucifer extracting worship through a network that rewards the best recruiters. What do you think?

Chapter 20

The First Ego

The theory I had laid out about Jesus being Lucifer's Messiah seemed to answer the impossible questions that had driven my investigation. By viewing Jesus through the theory that Lucifer was impersonating YHWH, I found that the contradictions in his character resolved into a coherent, if unsettling, picture. The biblical narrative appeared to fit this frame.

But a deeper disquiet began to stir. I had the sense that the scope of this drama was larger than I had outlined, that my findings represented but one layer of deception within a larger story.

My theory positioned Lucifer as the primary actor, the one who introduced a flaw into an otherwise perfect creation. But I failed to ask myself if Eden was ever perfect. I was resting on unfounded assumptions.

My attention was drawn back to the very beginning, to a question I had not yet asked: What does it truly mean to "know good and evil" in the biblical corpus?

In the ancient world, the ultimate authority of kings and gods was their right to judge. And to the ancient Jews, kings served as ultimate arbiters of justice.

To judge is to manipulate the perception of reality, to divide the world into the worthy and the unworthy, the righteous and the wicked, to have the final say on what it all means. It is the quintessential power of the Ego.

Thus, the tree of the knowledge of good and evil was considered the source of divine authority. It bestowed the power of the gods: the power to judge.

Suddenly, the Garden is no longer a paradise with a single flaw. It is a kingdom with a protected power source. Its creator, YHWH, is not just a father; he is a monarch guarding his authority.

I had always assumed that the serpent brought temptation into the Garden, but looking deeper, I could see that YHWH created it when he planted the tree. Notably, he placed it not in some distant corner, but in the very center, where it could not be missed.

And, as Bible readers have often asked, who created the serpent? YHWH. Isn't He responsible for his creations?

What if his command—"you must not eat of the tree of the knowledge of good and evil"—was designed to prevent his subjects from attaining the very power that defined him as God? This context gives us a viable motive. Why would YHWH create this temptation?

Isn't the judgment of good and evil really just a subjective conclusion, based on what someone thinks is right or wrong? Isn't reality just what it is, beyond all labels? The labels represent what we like and dislike, don't they?

If Elohim is the core of reality, and Elohim is All-That-Is—if Elohim is only Good, then there is no duality in actual fact.

The concept of opposition, of worthy versus unworthy, of good versus evil— maybe all of that comes from the tree. And the creator of the tree is YHWH.

In Genesis 1, we encounter Elohim—pure being, undivided reality. Elohim looks upon creation and sees that it is "good." But this isn't dualistic judgment. There's no comparison, no rejection, no division. Elohim simply recognizes the harmony of what is.

Then in Genesis 2, YHWH appears and plants the tree of the knowledge of good and evil. What if this tree doesn't contain moral knowledge, but the capacity to judge—to fragment the unified field of existence into opposing categories? Maybe this "fragmentation" is exactly what creates the "Voice of Accusation" (Satan) later on.

The Bible does not leave us to speculate. In the immediate aftermath of their eating from the tree, YHWH confesses his motive in his own words: "Yahweh God said, 'Behold, the man has become like one of us, knowing good and evil.

Now, lest he reach out his hand, and also take of the tree of life, and eat, and live forever--' therefore Yahweh God sent him out from the garden of Eden, to till the ground from which he was taken" (Gn 3:22-23).

Why would God be against humanity becoming an equal? It was a question I'd never before thought to ask. I read the words again and again.

"The man has become like one of us." Does this sound like a singular, all-powerful God?

It seems to me to be the voice of a king speaking to his court, a being who defines himself by his status. If so, then maybe he's motivated by fear that these new rivals, now judges, might also become immortal.

Beings who are his equal in power and in permanence are no longer subjects. They are potential competitors, aren't they?

Isn't this the raw, unveiled voice of Ego?

A secure, loving father would rejoice in the growth of their children, even hoping they might exceed him. Wouldn't you want that for your children?

What if the exile was not a punishment, but the strategic containment of potential rivals?

This analysis suggests that YHWH is the first Ego, and the tree represents his nature. And it reframes the tragedy of Lucifer as the perfect creation of this First Ego. He was a son made in his father's image, cursed with the same ambition.

What if Lucifer's fall was not a rebellion against a holy God, but an inevitable power struggle with a father operating from the same hierarchical framework—a secession, where Lucifer leaves the celestial court to establish his own rival kingdom: our world?

What if none of this was about actual good versus evil, which does not truly exist? Rather, could it simply describe different Egos competing for dominance? What if the tree introduced the capacity to divide reality into moral categories— and every being who ate from it, divine or human, became trapped in the same illusion of separation?

Just realizing this possibility required months of stripping away life-long assumptions about the Bible. I am not happy that the Jesus within the biblical

102

narrative might be Lucifer's Messiah, or that YHWH could be the birth of judgmental consciousness. It feels like a betrayal of the hope that set me on this path. And yet, if we play out the biblical narrative as if it were a true, cohesive whole—as biblical literalists and fundamentalist Christians insist we must—we find more evidence for the Kingdom of Ego than for the Kingdom of God.

The name itself supports this interpretation. When Moses asks for God's name at the burning bush, YHWH responds: 'I AM WHO I AM... tell them I AM has sent you' (Exodus 3:14). YHWH literally means 'I AM.' It's the emergence of the subjective 'I' that can observe and categorize. Isn't this the beginning of ego-consciousness?

When I refer to ego, I'm not suggesting something inherently wrong or evil. Ego is simply the subjective sense of being a differentiated person—the "I" that can have preferences, relationships, and experiences. When you say, "I love my child," that's ego expressing itself naturally. There's nothing inherently problematic about this.

Christianity supports my perspective through its insistence that YHWH is a personal God with whom you can have a personal relationship. The issue is that popular culture has demonized the word "ego" by defining it by its most extreme expressions like narcissism.

That line of thinking brings us back to YHWH's behavior. Throughout scripture, He demonstrates this extremely subjective perspective. He shows jealousy, fears competition, demands worship, and expresses wrath when he doesn't get what he wants. It seems to me that the pure, non-egoic source of being wouldn't behave this way.

This is even reflected in one of his most common titles. Do you remember how Yahweh (*YHWH Tzevaot*) described himself as the "God of Armies" in the passage from Isaiah that defines Lucifer? *Tzevaot* is often translated as "Lord of Hosts," but its primary meaning is martial: the Lord of War.

The implication of that title is staggering. A Lord of Armies can only exist in a universe of conflict. An undivided, non-dual Source has no enemies and needs no armies, does it?

This title seems to be the very definition of a being who operates from a place of "us versus them," a being trapped in the same pattern of judgment and separation as the Ego he condemns. It feels like the signature of a monarch, not the source of all being—at least to me.

If YHWH represents the beginning of ego and dualistic perception, what is Elohim? Imagine a being with no up or down, no right or left, no inner or outer. Imagine a being that has no opposite, beyond space and time. One with everything, but also somehow not of the universe, not of Eden. It is totally whole and complete unto itself, having no origin.

Isn't that Elohim?

But we can't even imagine this, for there is nothing in particular to lock the mind onto. Maybe YHWH, in part represents the polarizing opinions we entertain about ourselves, others, and what we call "reality." Maybe YHWH is that which perceives as a distinct being.

Maybe the original fracture wasn't in humanity, but in our misunderstanding or misperception of the Creator.

What do you think?

Part III

The Teachings

In Part II, our investigation led us down a dark path. Together, we followed the breadcrumbs of contradiction and manipulation to their source, uncovering a coherent and deeply unsettling pattern hiding in plain sight.

This is the point in the journey where it would be easy to feel despair, to close the book and conclude that the entire story is nothing but a trap.

But I must ask you to remember the promise that began this entire quest—the sorrowful figure in the childhood dream who said, "Find my bones. They are the core of my teaching. Most of what is written about me is untrue."

So, in Part III, "The Teachings," our work shifts. Having confronted the corruption, we now begin the excavation. Our question is no longer "What did Jesus do wrong?" but a far more vital one: "What did he teach that was so radical that it had to be buried beneath two millennia of theological deception?"

And here, a new and more subtle challenge awaits us. As we encounter teachings about our own divine nature, about unconditional love and forgiveness, about life everlasting—the temptation will be to cling to them. The natural impulse is to create a "Good Jesus" to rescue us from the "Bad Jesus" we just met.

I admit, this was my own struggle in writing this book. My heart wanted to find a hero I could save from the wreckage. But creating a new, comfortable story is just another form of blindness.

We are not here to choose a side, but to continue our work as detectives, seeing the whole, complex, and contradictory picture without flinching.

Chapter 21

The Immortals

What I'd discovered about YHWH left me questioning everything I thought I knew about Abrahamic religions. I had fundamentally misunderstood their basis my entire life, and what I was seeing now was far more biblically grounded and far darker than any of my previous conceptions of the biblical narrative.

As I sat in that uncomfortable silence, something kept nagging me: the promise I'd made as an eight-year-old boy, standing before that boneless figure in my dreams, who said, "Find my bones. They are the core of my teaching. Most of what is written about me is untrue. Mankind has twisted my message for selfish gain, until almost nothing of its essence remains."

That thought sparked a flint of hope---maybe there was still something left to learn.

Maybe the very contradictions I'd been documenting were proof of this claim. Maybe there were two completely different sources at work in these texts.

I had to keep digging, not despite my revulsion, but because of it. If something this dark could masquerade as divine for millennia, then finding whatever authentic teaching might remain was essential.

So I returned to the Gospels with a different question: Instead of asking "What did Jesus do wrong?" I began asking, "What did he teach that was so radical it had to be obscured?"

What I found completely transformed my understanding of Jesus's biblical teachings. The same man who delayed while his friend died had also taught some of the most astonishing ideas I'd ever encountered—teachings so extreme that they seemed to come from an entirely different source.

These teachings had been there all along, but I'd been so focused on the contradictions that I'd missed their monumental implications. I felt I had to follow the trail. So, for the time being, let's step back from Jesus's storyline and enter the rabbit hole to see where these unexpected teachings take us. We'll return to the narrative later.

Throughout the Gospels, Jesus is referred to as the Son of God. That was my first clue. I didn't really know what that meant.

As a child, I'd been taught this meant Jesus was uniquely divine—God's only Son. But something nagged at me. I thought it might be a clue.

I started searching through scripture for how that phrase, "Son of God," was used. What I found made me stop and reread the passage. Could this really be what it seemed to say?

The phrase "Son of God" wasn't unique to Jesus. Though saying this was prohibited in Jesus's day, due to Caesar claiming that title, in ancient Hebrew tradition, it referred to kings, prophets, even entire communities.

Then I found John 10. Jesus is accused of blasphemy for saying, "I and the Father are one." The religious leaders pick up stones to kill him. His response challenged everything I had been taught as a child.

Jesus responded by pointing to their own scriptures: "Isn't it written in your law, 'I said, you are gods'?" He was quoting Psalm 82, where God calls humans "gods." Jesus argued that if their own scripture calls people gods, it was not blasphemy for him to call himself the Son of God.

I suppose it makes sense when you consider that according to Genesis, we are the creations of God—his children. I fumbled for Psalm 82, the passage Jesus was quoting to verify the statement. Indeed, it said exactly what Jesus claimed.

My body jolted upright. Both the Old and New Testaments say we are gods! Weren't we taught that Jesus was uniquely divine? But here wasn't he using their own scripture to show them that we are all sons and daughters of God?

The implications were staggering. The Psalm continues: "Nevertheless you shall die like men, and fall like one of the rulers."

What? I'd never heard anything like this from pastors.

I kept reading, looking for more. What else had Jesus said that I'd missed? That's when I found many verses I'd never heard preached the way Jesus seemed to mean them.

"Most certainly, I tell you, if a person keeps my word, he will never see death" (Jn 8:51).

Never see death? I read it again. Not will have eternal life in heaven. But will *never see death.* Present tense. Physical. Certainty.

The Jews listening to Jesus responded, "Now we know that you have a demon. Abraham died, and the prophets; and you say, 'If a man keeps my word, he will never taste of death.'" They thought he was possessed, so radical was the idea!

They knew he was talking about physical death, not some other-dimensional life.

I didn't begin this project with the belief that Jesus was teaching *physical immortality.* But the more I read, the more evidence I found. Consider the following:

"For God so loved the world, that he gave his only born Son, that whoever believes in him should not perish, but have eternal life" (Jn 3:16).

"Most certainly I tell you, he who hears my word and believes him who sent me has eternal life, and doesn't come into judgment, but has passed out of death into life" (Jn 5:24).

How had I failed to notice these verses before? Every sermon I'd ever heard about eternal life focused on the afterlife. But Jesus was talking about not dying at all.

And, as I read on, I found more.

"My sheep hear my voice, and I know them, and they follow me. I give eternal life to them. They will never perish, and no one will snatch them out of my hand" (Jn 10:27–28).

I found the conversation with Martha at Lazarus's tomb extremely revealing: "Jesus said to her, 'I am the resurrection and the life. He who believes in me will still live, even if he dies. Whoever lives and believes in me will never die. Do you believe this?'" (Jn 11:25–26).

There it was again, as Jesus raised to life a man three days dead. Will never die. Not metaphorically. Not spiritually. *Never* die.

And it's not just the Book of John that's talking physical immortality.

"These will go away into eternal punishment, but the righteous into eternal life" (Mt 25:46).

"For they can't die any more, for they are like the angels and are children of God, being children of the resurrection" (Lk 20:36).

I looked back to the opening chapters of the Old Testament. There I found the same teaching in Genesis 3. The earlier text indicates that Adam and Eve were immortal until they ate from the tree of the knowledge of good and evil.

Looking beyond the story of Eden in the Old Testament, I found reference to immortality in Proverbs as well: "In the way of righteousness is life; in its path there is no death" (Prv 12:28).

Immortality.

The more I dug, the more I realized just how strongly Jesus, and early Christianity, emphasized the physical nature of this promise. After his resurrection, he went out of his way to prove he wasn't just a spirit: "See my hands and my feet, that it is truly me. Touch me and see, for a spirit doesn't have flesh and bones, as you see that I have" (Lk 24:39).

You are probably thinking, *"Didn't we already establish that the resurrection accounts are unreliable?"*

Yes. I am not referencing these stories to prove they are historically true. I am referencing them as forensic evidence of a belief system. The very fact that the Gospel writers felt it was necessary to include these specific, physical details—eating fish, touching wounds—proves that the original promise was about physical immortality. They were trying to convince their audience that a real body had returned from the grave.

I sat there staring at my notes. Page after page of verses I'd never heard preached in *this way*. Verses pastors typically described as metaphor or relegated to some distant future.

But what if Jesus meant literal immortality?

He was saying something the Pharisees couldn't accept: We are immortal gods, and we have forgotten that fact.

Was this the faith he was constantly referring to? That we are immortals?

To understand how radical these promises were, we need to grasp what Jesus's Jewish audience expected about death and resurrection.

Traditional Jewish theology, rooted in passages like Daniel 12:2, taught that the righteous would die and then be raised bodily at the Day of Judgment: "Many of those who sleep in the dust of the earth shall awake, some to everlasting life, and some to shame and everlasting contempt."

This resurrection was physical—real bodies returning to life—but it came after death. People would die, be buried properly to preserve their remains, and then be raised when God established his kingdom on earth. Even the most faithful expected to experience death before resurrection.

But it seems, Jesus was promising something unprecedented: that believers could skip death entirely. When he said followers would "never see death" or "never taste death," he wasn't just talking about resurrection after dying. He was claiming people could achieve continuous immortality while still living.

The distinction was crucial. Post-Babylonian Jewish resurrection theology offered hope after death. Jesus offered escape from death itself. No Hebrew prophet had made such promises. Even figures like Enoch and Elijah, who were said to have been taken up to heaven alive, were considered exceptional cases, not examples of what ordinary Jews could achieve.

This context makes the Pharisees' incredulous response understandable. They knew that theology. They were rejecting an entirely new category of promise that went beyond anything in their scriptural tradition.

But there was another clue about Jesus and his physical immortality teachings.

Jesus kept referring to himself as the "Son of Man," which I had assumed was a divine title. When I looked up the Hebrew, I found that "Son of Man" means exactly what it appears to mean—a human being.

In Hebrew, *ben adam* is not a unique title; it literally means "Son of Adam." Since biblically we are all descendants of Adam, the phrase applies to every single human being. But the meaning goes even deeper. The name *Adam* is derived from *adamah*, which means "ground" or "soil." So, *ben adam* essentially means "Son of the Soil"—a creature made of dirt.

That's you. That's me.

Even in the book of Ezekiel, God kept calling the prophet "son of man"—emphasizing his humanity, not his specialness.

In Daniel 7:13–14, a "son of man" receives divine authority and power. But if this phrase just means "human being," then wasn't Jesus saying that any human, when properly aligned, could access that same divine authority?

Was he demonstrating what we're all capable of, rather than what made him unique?

Then I found still another clue in the Gospel of Mark:

"These signs will accompany those who believe: in my name they will cast out demons; they will speak with new tongues; they will take up serpents; and if they drink any deadly thing, it will in no way hurt them; they will lay hands on the sick, and they will recover" (Mk 16:17–18).

Jesus promised believers would be completely immune to snake venom and poison!

I had read this many times before, but I never took it seriously. I once saw a documentary on a sect of Christianity that practices this.

Pentecostal serpent handling churches, primarily centered in the Southern U.S., but also represented in the Midwest and in large East Coast states like Pennsylvania, handle venomous rattlesnakes and copperheads during worship services as a demonstration of faith.

Researching these churches, I noticed something curious. They handle snakes regularly, but they rarely drink poison. Same verse, same promise, but they're selective about which part they practice.

When I dug deeper, I found that members of these churches who have drunk poison—strychnine, specifically—have died.

What did this mean?

Here were people who claim absolute belief in Jesus's promises. But when they drank poison, they died.

Of course, sometimes practitioners are bitten by their snakes too, but only on rare occasions do members die. Most people bitten by rattlesnakes and copperheads do not die, regardless of their beliefs.

Vipers can regulate how much venom they deliver. Their survival depends on conserving venom for prey they will eat. Thus, many human bites convey very little or no venom.

In the event of envenomation, even without medical treatment, there is about an 80% survival rate. Most healthy adults will survive rattlesnake or copperhead bites. With medical treatment, 99.8% of adults survive.

But poison—you get the dose you take.

My mind flashed back to the temptations in the desert. One of the temptations was to test faith, which Jesus warned against, quoting Deuteronomy 6:16, "It is also written: 'Do not put the Lord your God to the test.'"

Was this another contradiction? How could Jesus tell us that the faithful will do these things and also warn against testing God? I found this confusing.

The scripture about serpent handling, poison, casting out demons and laying on of hands stated that faith was essential. This sparked my curiosity about the meaning of faith and belief.

Do the Pentecostals demonstrate faith or belief through their snake handling? Both?

What if belief and faith aren't the same thing?

In a marriage, being faithful doesn't mean believing your partner exists. It means actions in alignment with your commitment: faithful behavior, consistency, integrity.

What if Jesus's promises required not just belief, but perfect alignment with the commandments he taught? Love universally and unconditionally. Judge not. Forgive absolutely. Be completely sinless.

The serpent handlers might have complete belief that they will be protected, but have they been perfectly faithful to Jesus's actual requirements? Has anyone?

I realized I couldn't use cases of their deaths to prove anything about Jesus's statements. Maybe there are very stringent standards to meet before realizing one's immortality.

If belief alone were sufficient to achieve this status, why did Jesus teach Love, non-judgment, and forgiveness so vigorously? Why did he scorn those who believed but did not follow the practices?

"Not everyone who says to me, 'Lord, Lord,' will enter into the Kingdom of Heaven, but he who does the will of my Father who is in heaven. Many will tell me in that day, 'Lord, Lord, didn't we prophesy in your name, in your name cast out demons, and in your name do many mighty works?' Then I will tell them, 'I never knew you. Depart from me, you who work iniquity'" (Mt 7:21-23).

Maybe belief alone isn't sufficient. Maybe you'd need perfect alignment with God. Maybe that's why Jesus described the path as straight and narrow and why he stressed love, forgiveness, and non-judgment so relentlessly.

This raises an obvious question that might be troubling you: If Jesus really believed his followers could achieve immortality and "never see death," why did he tell them to "take up their cross" and prepare for crucifixion? Why would he orchestrate his own crucifixion if he had transcended death?

The answer may lie in understanding his crucifixion as a strategic demonstration rather than a contradiction.

From a Jewish theological perspective, crucifixion represented the ultimate spiritual catastrophe—being marked as cursed by God, denied proper burial, and excluded from resurrection. As we explored in our interlude on crucifixion, this meant permanent separation from God and the community of the faithful.

If Jesus genuinely believed his immortality teachings worked, then proving they could overcome even crucifixion would be the ultimate validation. Maybe he wasn't asking followers to accept what he wouldn't accept himself. Maybe his aim was to demonstrate that perfect spiritual alignment could transcend any supposed separation from God.

This explains his emphasis after resurrection on proving his body was physical. He ate fish, let Thomas touch his wounds, showed his flesh and bones.

The crucifixion becomes proof of concept: if the method worked even under these extreme circumstances, all followers could have confidence in their immortality.

Imagine it—hundreds or thousands of Christians rising from the dead on the same day Jesus arose. It would be the ultimate wakeup call!

Whether this demonstration validated his teaching or simply created a powerful psychological narrative is another question entirely.

Regarding physical immortality, so much scripture supports it as being Jesus's primary teaching. Yet, despite the overwhelming evidence, Christianity does not teach this promise of physical immortality, even Pentecostal snake-handlers.

Maybe no one has the eyes to see and the ears to hear. Or maybe no one really takes Jesus at his word. Maybe even the most faithful are highly selective in their beliefs.

And immortality is hard to believe, considering we have no verifiable record of anyone living beyond 120 or so years. It's no wonder the Pharisees were incredulous. Again, everything I thought I understood about Jesus and the Bible was up in the air.

Author's Note: *Physical resurrection was a core Jewish belief in Jesus's time and remains so for Orthodox Jews today. Early Christians expected it immediately, as Matthew's zombie scene demonstrates. Religious leaders thought Jesus was possessed not because he taught resurrection—they believed that too—but because he claimed there was a way to never die. If Christians believe Jesus is God, why do they deny his Word about physical resurrection and physical immortality?*

Chapter 22

The Eunuchs

While researching immortality in the last chapter, I discovered another discordant piece of the narrative, so glaring that I was baffled as to how I had missed it before.

After learning about the zombie rising at the end of Matthew, understanding Jewish beliefs about physical resurrection, and realizing it's possible Jesus did not actually resurrect based on the contradictory accounts and the complete absence of his rising in the oldest versions of Mark, I found myself staring at teachings that seemed completely at odds with Christianity as we know it.

Jesus appeared to be teaching that marriage was incompatible with immortality. This seems to fly in the face of everything we've been taught about Christian family values: the emphasis on marriage as God's design, the blessing of children, the sanctity of the nuclear family.

But there it was, verse after verse, impossible to ignore once I started connecting them. The first passage I found was in Matthew 19:10, where Jesus discusses divorce with the Pharisees. After giving strict rules about marriage, his disciples respond that if divorce is so difficult, "it is not expedient to marry."

Jesus's response was startling: "Not all men can receive this saying, but those to whom it is given. For there are eunuchs who were born that way from their mother's womb, and there are eunuchs who were made eunuchs by men; and there are eunuchs who made themselves eunuchs for the Kingdom of Heaven's sake. He who is able to receive it, let him receive it" (Mt 19:11-12).

Eunuchs for the Kingdom of Heaven's sake? What does that mean?

Then I found the passage that made the connection explicit. When questioned about marriage in the afterlife, Jesus said: "The children of this age marry and are given in marriage. But those who are considered worthy to attain to that age and the resurrection from the dead neither marry nor are given in marriage. For they can't die any more, for they are like the angels and are children of God, being children of the resurrection" (Lk 20:34-36).

I read this again and again. Those "worthy" of resurrection—the immortal state where "they can't die any more"—neither marry nor are given in marriage.

The parallel passage in Matthew was equally clear: "For in the resurrection they neither marry nor are given in marriage, but are like God's angels in heaven" (Mt 22:30).

Seeking clarity, I began researching the prophets to see their attitudes toward marriage and family. Though many were celibate, they did not teach that others should be. Examples include John the Baptist, Ezekiel, Jeremiah, and Daniel.

The closest parallel might be Elijah, who was celibate and lived outside normal social structures, and who was said to have been taken up to heaven alive, achieving the immortality Jesus taught about. However, Elijah doesn't explicitly teach against marriage for others.

Maybe Jesus had an insight into Elijah's life that is not recorded. In any case, Jesus's systematic opposition to family structures seems quite unique among biblical prophets. Most prophets were married (Isaiah, Hosea, Ezekiel before his wife's death) and didn't present celibacy as essential to salvation.

I found myself thinking about Genesis. In Genesis 1:28, God commands humans to "be fruitful and multiply." However, Jesus's teachings about celibacy and family detachment seem to contradict this original divine mandate. I'm uncertain how to reconcile these apparent contradictions within the biblical narrative.

If immortality requires celibacy, and marriage prevents immortality, then marriage would lead to death, wouldn't it? Jesus's comment that "not all men can receive this saying" acknowledges how difficult this teaching would be to accept.

It's an astonishing claim, but the texts are clear that those worthy of resurrection "neither marry nor are given in marriage" because "they are like the angels."

116

The connection between celibacy and immortality appears consistently across these passages.

Suddenly, I felt I was not taking Jesus's words seriously enough, which is what we are taught to do by Fundamentalist Christianity. It's what I promised to do at the outset of this book.

I had to try harder to piece together these teachings, as would a sincere investigator. Doing this, I encountered something I hadn't expected: the logic simply wouldn't hold together, and the harder I tried to make sense of it, the more psychologically strained I felt, especially if I imagined everything Jesus taught was true. Let me show you what I mean.

If the price of marriage is death, as Jesus states, you'd expect him to encourage divorce as a remedy. Instead, he speaks against divorce and treats remarriage as adultery. This creates a trap where marriage dooms you with no escape.

This theological bind has trapped many Christians in guilt and shame—some remaining in harmful marriages believing divorce damns them, others divorcing but living with religious guilt, not realizing that, according to Jesus, *they cannot enter the kingdom of heaven.*

If you are feeling a sense of suffocation or panic reading this logic, pay attention to that feeling. It may be the sound of a trap snapping shut.

Even more puzzling: Jesus elsewhere said, "let the dead bury their dead," seemingly dismissing concerns about mortal affairs. But if married people are spiritually dead according to his immortality teachings, why give them detailed rules about divorce at all? Shouldn't his response be to dismiss such concerns entirely?

The contradictions multiplied the more I examined them. If you're already mortal due to marriage, divorce wouldn't make you any more mortal. The logical teaching would be: "Never marry if you want immortality. If you're already married, you've chosen mortality, so divorce is irrelevant to your spiritual state."

I found myself experiencing something I hadn't anticipated: trying to rationalize these fundamentally contradictory teachings was disorienting. The harder I worked to make them coherent, the more confused I became. There's something genuinely unsettling about prolonged exposure to illogical thought patterns.

At some point, I recognized the problem wasn't my comprehension, but the material itself. Sometimes the most honest response to genuinely incoherent teachings is to recognize them as incoherent rather than exhaust yourself trying to solve unsolvable contradictions.

This may explain the vast machinery of Christian apologetics—the formal discipline, taught in seminaries, where leaders are trained to defend the faith against objections.

Rather than acknowledge the logical impossibilities, the approach seems to be changing Jesus's meaning until the contradictions disappear or punting with "God works in mysterious ways." But doing so abandons the methodology of taking the texts seriously as they were written, which is what fundamentalists and literalists insist we do.

Here's what gives me pause about taking this literally: Jesus also taught that saints would physically rise from the dead, as described in Matthew's zombie scene, yet this clearly didn't happen as described. If Jesus was wrong about physical resurrection occurring in his lifetime, then perhaps his teachings about achieving immortality—including the requirements for it—were also based on false assumptions about human potential.

This realization allows us to appreciate these passages as biblical artifacts of first-century religious thought without feeling compelled to follow teachings that may have been fundamentally mistaken.

Many fundamentalist Christians selectively apply biblical teachings while claiming the Bible is flawless. They might justify this through interpretive frameworks, but these frameworks still require subjective decisions about which passages apply literally.

If the Bible were truly the perfect word of God, such elaborate interpretation wouldn't be necessary—the truth would be self-evident. The need for sophisticated systems to explain away contradictions suggests Christians implicitly recognize the Bible is not the flawless document they claim it to be.

Interlude:

The Forbidden Knowledge

While scouring my Bible for more on the immortality teachings of Jesus, I found references to Enoch being raised to heaven alive (Heb 11:5) and quotations of his prophecies by Jesus's brother, Jude, in the Book of Jude (1:14–15).

After some research, I discovered that the Book of Enoch, not found in the Bible, clearly influenced the early Christian worldview. Given these canonical references to Enochian teachings, examining this context becomes necessary to more fully understand Jesus's teachings.

The book describes fallen angels who share evil or forbidden knowledge with humanity. Much of the technology they taught, we take for granted as being the very foundations of civilization.

Author's Note: *The Book of Enoch, while not in the biblical canon, is readily available in various translations for those interested in examining these teachings directly.*

According to Enoch, angels called "Watchers" taught metalworking for weapons and tools; cosmetics and jewelry for vanity; the courses of the sun, moon, and stars for navigation and timekeeping; weather signs for agriculture; medicinal plants for healing; and various forms of knowledge about the natural world.

To modern readers, the idea that these categories of knowledge are evil might seem absurd. But that may be precisely the point. Every one of these "forbidden" teachings has evolved into the technological systems we depend on today.

Consider what metallurgy alone has become: not just weapons and tools, but the entire technological infrastructure of modern life. Every computer chip, every car, every building's frame, every electrical wire, every medical device, every satellite—all depend on metallurgy.

Without metalworking, there would be no industrial revolution, no electronics, no modern medicine, no transportation systems, no communications networks. The "forbidden knowledge" of working with metals became the skeleton of technological civilization itself.

Cosmetics became the beauty industry and social media filters; astronomical knowledge became GPS and satellite technology; weather signs became meteorology and climate modeling; root-cutting became pharmaceuticals and industrial agriculture. We've built our entire global civilization on what these texts identify as corrupting knowledge that traps us in mortality.

According to Enochian tradition, these technologies were forbidden because humans were meant to develop dormant capacities that would make them equal to angels—immortal beings with direct divine connection. Jewish mystical tradition teaches that Enoch, a human, was transformed into Metatron, one of the highest angels, without dying.

The Book of Enoch argues that sharing this knowledge is evil because we are developing angels and just don't realize it. Thus, providing us with these external shortcuts prevents us from discovering our hidden potential. Imagine if this were true—you are a developing angel and just don't realize it.

This context illuminates Jesus's radical teachings: "You are gods" (Jn 10:34), promises that his followers will "never see death" (Jn 8:51), and his insistence that the resurrected "can't die anymore, for they are like the angels" (Lk 20:36).

His call to abandon all civilizational supports—possessions, planning, family structures—may represent the same fundamental choice: develop external technologies that keep us trapped in mortality, or discover the internal capacities that reveal our divine nature.

It seems both The Book of Enoch and the Gospels suggest humanity faces this stark choice: external dependence that trades short-term physical survival for ultimate death, or the path of trust that transforms us into immortal gods.

Are we unrealized angels? Gods?

Chapter 23

The Word

Let's imagine Jesus's immortality teachings were true and ask the intriguing questions. If we took seriously his assertion that "you are gods," what would that imply about human capabilities? If we are gods, what are our powers, and how do we activate them?

Those questions took me down the ultimate rabbit hole.

I remembered a verse that stuck with me since I was a child. It was this startling promise Jesus made to his disciples: "Most certainly I tell you, he who believes in me, the works that I do, he will do also; and he will do greater works than these, because I am going to my Father" (Jn 14:12).

What did Jesus mean by greater works? And how had we all missed this?

If Jesus walked on water, what would be greater? If he healed the sick, what would surpass that? If he raised the dead, what could be more powerful?

I also remembered the mountain passage. Jesus didn't just teach about the power of words. He taught about combining words with faith.

When his disciples asked why they could not cast out certain demons, he said to them, "Because of your unbelief. For most certainly I tell you, if you have faith as a grain of mustard seed, you will tell this mountain, 'Move from here to there,' and it will move; and nothing will be impossible for you" (Mt 17:20).

Move a mountain? Surely he was using hyperbole to make a point about the creative power we've forgotten we possess, right? But the pattern is clear. According to Jesus, a combination of faith, the content of one's heart, and the spoken word created a reality-shaping power.

I realize how this sounds. But here it was, verse after verse, in the most traditional religious text. The more I searched, the more I found.

Remember when he said the "Son of Man" will inherit the Kingdom of Heaven?

I was starting to get the sense that there were two versions of Jesus. One version of Jesus was saying *he* will inherit the Kingdom of Heaven, while the other Jesus was saying that any human, when properly aligned, could access that same divine authority. That thought was staggering.

The inclusive version of Jesus seemed to be suggesting that *our* words—ordinary human words—may be central to exercising our divine authority. It's an astonishing thought. Watch for it, won't you?

Scripture was full of references to the creative power of speech: "Death and life are in the power of the tongue; those who love it will eat its fruit" (Prv 18:21).

And "There is one who speaks rashly like the piercing of a sword, but the tongue of the wise heals" (Prv 12:18).

If we really were gods with amnesia, then our words would have creative power, wouldn't they?

That's a scary thought, when I think about all the things that have come out of my mouth over the years! So, I began searching for his teachings about our words.

Even God seemed to take words seriously: "I tell you that every idle word that men speak, they will give account of it in the day of judgment. For by your words you will be justified, and by your words you will be condemned" (Mt 12:36-37).

Every word? That seems extreme. But I found more: "The good man out of the good treasure of his heart brings out that which is good, and the evil man out of the evil treasure of his heart brings out that which is evil, for out of the abundance of the heart, his mouth speaks" (Lk 6:45).

Also, "That which enters into the mouth doesn't defile the man; but that which proceeds out of the mouth, this defiles the man" (Mt 15:11).

Then I found the key that connected everything: "In the beginning was the Word, and the Word was with God, and the Word was God" (Jn 1:1).

So, according to the Book of John, the Word is the directive force of reality itself. And, it seems, Jesus said we wield that same power.

I thought about Genesis and how God spoke creation into existence. Let there be light: the Word creating reality.

Was Jesus saying that we do the same thing? There is so much scripture saying that our words bless or curse, build up or tear down.

Why do so many churches obfuscate these teachings?

Then I found James, Jesus's brother, discussing the power of the tongue: "And the tongue is a fire. The world of iniquity among our members is the tongue, which defiles the whole body, and sets on fire the course of nature, and is set on fire by Gehenna" (Jas 3:6).

What if these teachings were true? What if we really are gods who create with our words, who transcend death through proper alignment with the Word?

Most sobering of all is the possibility we've been speaking ourselves and our loved ones into death every single day, not realizing the power we wield.

I sat in silence, feeling the weight of these teachings. It seemed to me that these teachings of Jesus all pointed in the same direction: We are more than we know. And our words are the key to remembering, or forgetting, what we are.

Author's Note: *These biblical passages about the creative power of words remind me of the modern "law of attraction" teachings found in New Age thinking, something many Christians claim to be of the occult. I wonder if readers will notice the similarity and what they might make of it.*

Like the immortality promises we examined earlier, these claims about word-power seem to make empirical assertions about how reality works. Whether such ideas function as described or represent another set of first-century beliefs that don't match observable experience, is something each reader will need to evaluate for themselves.

Chapter 24

The Second Exodus

Jesus's idea that we are immortal gods who have forgotten our nature seemed so fundamental that I had to retrace my Bible journey to revisit his earliest teachings. That brought me to the Sermon on the Mount, which I reread with totally new eyes. What I found made me realize just how much I had missed in my previous Bible study.

I've read the Sermon on the Mount dozens of times. It was familiar and inspiring. It seemed like Jesus at his most gentle and wise, though I don't think I ever truly understood it.

However, after seeing Jesus's teachings of physical immortality, about us being gods, I opened to Matthew 5 and started with the Beatitudes, expecting the unexpected.

"Blessed are the poor in spirit, for theirs is the Kingdom of Heaven." I paused. Poor in spirit. Not the wealthy, successful, confident people. But the humble ones. Those of us who are not very willful?

"Blessed are those who mourn, for they shall be comforted." Those who have lost family? The Jesus that uttered this seems at odds with the Jesus who said we are to hate our families, and that we should let the dead bury their dead. What's going on here? I don't know.

"Blessed are the meek, for they shall inherit the earth." The meek. Not the aggressive, competitive ones. The gentle souls.

Maybe Jesus wasn't talking to everyone. It seemed he was talking to *a very specific type of person.*

The Second Exodus

The people who *couldn't* make it in dog-eat-dog society: the sensitive ones, those too gentle to thrive in competitive systems, the ones who get trampled.

"Blessed are those who hunger and thirst for righteousness, for they shall be filled." People who care about what's right, not what's profitable?

"Blessed are the merciful, for they shall obtain mercy." The compassionate ones who get taken advantage of?

"Blessed are the pure in heart, for they shall see God." The innocent people? The dreamers?

"Blessed are the peacemakers, for they shall be called children of God." People who try to resolve conflict rather than dominate?

He was identifying his target audience, wasn't he? Aren't these the personality types who tend to get crushed in aggressive societies?

Are you one of those people who can't bring yourself to be ruthless? Who gets pushed around because you don't push back? Maybe Jesus was talking to people like you.

But then I kept reading and found some hiccups.

"You have heard that it was said, 'An eye for an eye, and a tooth for a tooth.' But I tell you, don't resist him who is evil; but whoever strikes you on your right cheek, turn to him the other also." Do not resist. Anyone. Ever.

What if we had tried that with Hitler? Realistically, wouldn't people take total advantage of you if you had no boundaries?

"If anyone sues you to take away your coat, let him have your cloak also." Give them more than they ask for.

"Whoever compels you to go one mile, go with him two." Do twice as much as demanded.

"Give to him who asks you, and don't turn away him who desires to borrow from you." My stomach dropped. Give to everyone who asks? You'd be cleaned out in no time.

Unless you were immortal and could use the Word to manifest whatever you needed for survival—then these teachings would make sense.

"You have heard that it was said, 'You shall love your neighbor and hate your enemy.' But I tell you, love your enemies, bless those who curse you, do good to those who hate you, and pray for those who mistreat you and persecute you." Love the people trying to destroy you.

Who could live this way?

I read fervently. And then reread. How had I missed this before?

"Don't lay up treasures for yourselves on the earth, where moth and rust consume, and where thieves break through and steal." Don't save anything. Don't plan for the future. Have no home.

"Therefore, I tell you, don't be anxious for your life: what you will eat, or what you will drink; nor yet for your body, what you will wear." Don't worry about survival, at all.

"See the birds of the sky, that they don't sow, neither do they reap, nor gather into barns. Your heavenly Father feeds them." Live like the birds. No planning. No storing. No external security.

"But seek first God's Kingdom and his righteousness; and all these things will be given to you as well." Focus only on divine alignment. Everything else will be provided.

I had to pause. This no longer seemed like simple advice for gentle souls. This seemed to be a complete exit strategy from civilization itself.

Wasn't this the Second Exodus?

Moses had led the Israelites out of physical slavery in Egypt. What if Jesus was leading gentle souls out of the spiritual slavery of society?

Moses said: Come out of Egypt. Maybe Jesus was saying: *Come out of the whole system.*

Moses led them into the wilderness where God provided manna. Jesus taught: Don't worry about food—God will provide.

Moses spent forty years in the wilderness. Jesus spent forty days in the wilderness.

The parallel was perfect. But this time, the slavery wasn't physical. Maybe it was the bondage of trying to survive in systems that made you ungodly.

If that was what Jesus meant, the Promised Land wasn't a physical location or territory, but *immortal consciousness.*

Who could live this way?

These teachings were not only impossible for individuals unless we are gods; they were completely incompatible with any existing form of civilization.

No resistance to evil? You can't have laws or police. Give to everyone who asks? You can't have property or economics. Don't store treasures? You can't have savings or planning. Love your enemies and turn the other cheek? You can't have military or defense.

The gentle souls he was recruiting had to choose: stay in the competitive system that was crushing them or follow him into total social exile.

And it would only work if you lived in perfect alignment with your immortal nature. It would only work if you really could create reality with your words. Otherwise, wasn't it suicide?

You might think, "Wasn't Jesus talking about monastic life?" That's a common Christian interpretation. But Christian monasticism didn't develop until 2-3 centuries later.

Considering it more deeply, I saw that living in a monastery is in no way synonymous with living like birds. Monasteries have rules, hierarchies, and structure. Monasteries are dependent upon society for financial support.

What about begging? That was the path of the monk before the advent of monasteries. But just like monasteries, beggars depend on society.

I flipped to Matthew 7, in anticipation of what it would reveal. "Therefore be perfect, even as your Father in heaven is perfect." Be perfect. Not try harder. Be perfect.

But how? The Greek word here is *teleios,* which means complete or mature. But in the context of "as your Father in heaven is perfect," the standard is divine wholeness. How can a human achieve divine wholeness unless that wholeness is already our nature?

Jesus was teaching something that sounded remarkably like the teachings of John the Baptist, so I read about John.

As I read, I could see Jesus wasn't speaking into a vacuum.

Right before Jesus began teaching, John the Baptist had drawn massive crowds with exactly the same message: "Then people from Jerusalem, all of Judea, and all the region around the Jordan went out to him" (Mt 3:5-6).

And what was John teaching? Complete civilization exit.

But why did such massive crowds respond to this call for wilderness living? It seems they recognized something ancient returning.

When Jesus later told his disciples that John was the Elijah who was to come before the Messiah (Mt 11:14), he was confirming what many already sensed, the revival of a prophetic tradition stretching back over a thousand years.

Elijah had lived the same way: no possessions, relying on divine provision, confronting corrupt authority, living in the wilderness in complete independence. And Elijah, like Enoch, had been taken up to heaven alive, achieving exactly what Jesus would later teach about immortality.

So, from the perspective of the people, this may not have been a radical new teaching. Maybe they were embracing the return of their greatest independence prophet.

This explains John's appearance and way of life: "Now John himself wore clothing made of camel's hair with a leather belt around his waist. His food was locusts and wild honey" (Mt 3:4).

John lived in the wilderness with no possessions, no family, no institutional support. He called people to abandon the entire system.

Contrary to what we might assume, the people didn't think he was crazy. Instead, they considered him a true prophet of God.

But why?

Thousands of people so desired this path that they left their homes to live on insects and honey in the desert. Think about that. What must the living conditions have been like to make living hand to mouth in the wilderness appealing?

When John offered wilderness life, he was offering escape from crushing taxation, brutal occupation, religious corruption, and economic exploitation.

Weren't these masses the gentle souls Jesus identified? To them, eating locusts may have represented liberation.

Jesus openly supported John's teachings, later telling the religious leaders: "For John came to you in the way of righteousness, and you didn't believe him; but the tax collectors and the prostitutes believed him. When you saw it, you didn't even repent afterward, that you might believe him" (Mt 21:32).

So, from their perspective, Jesus may not have been delivering an impossible dream, but completing a mass-liberation movement, where people were willing to sacrifice everything to join.

I could see that the Sermon on the Mount was the operating manual for the Second Exodus. From civilization to God consciousness: this way of living was for gentle souls who couldn't make it in aggressive systems anyway.

But then I found a story that brought the Second Exodus into sharp focus. A rich young ruler approaches Jesus and asks what he must do to inherit eternal life.

Jesus tells him to follow the commandments. The young man says he's kept them all since youth. Then comes Jesus's response: "One thing you lack. Go, sell whatever you have and give to the poor, and you will have treasure in heaven; and come, follow me, taking up the cross" (Mt 19:21).

The young man walks away sad, because he has great wealth.

Then Jesus turns to his disciples: "Most certainly I say to you, a rich man will enter into the Kingdom of Heaven with difficulty. Again I tell you, it is easier for a camel to enter in through a needle's eye than for a rich man to enter into God's Kingdom" (Mt 19:23-24).

A camel through a needle's eye? Impossible. Jesus's disciples agreed: "When the disciples heard it, they were exceedingly astonished, saying, 'Who then can be saved?'"

"Jesus, looking at them, said, 'With men this is impossible, but with God all things are possible'" (Mt 19:26).

Maybe I understood. The rich young ruler represented everyone too invested in the competitive system to follow the exodus path. He couldn't let go of the very structure that was crushing the gentle souls Jesus was trying to lead out. Can you truly exit civilization while maintaining your stake in it?

Jesus had been explicit about this impossibility. He'd said plainly: "No one can serve two masters, for either he will hate the one and love the other, or else he will be devoted to one and despise the other. You can't serve God and Mammon" (Mt 6:24).

The way he presents it makes it sound like a law of consciousness. You're either in the system, or you're out. The rich young ruler discovered he couldn't do both.

The Pharisees' reaction to Jesus's teaching about money was revealing: "The Pharisees, who were lovers of money, also heard all these things, and they scoffed at him" (Lk 16:14).

I paused. Aren't we today just as invested in the monetary system as were those who scoffed?

Jesus's response was devastating: "He said to them, 'You are those who justify yourselves in the sight of men, but God knows your hearts. For that which is exalted among men is an abomination in the sight of God'" (Lk 16:15).

According to Jesus, virtually everything we prize today—wealth, status, power, security—was anathema to the Kingdom of Heaven. Maybe this explained why so few could follow the path. It demanded detachment from *everything*.

I continued reading, and I was surprised to see Jesus's seemingly simplistic interpretation of wealth.

Jesus told a story about a rich man and a beggar named Lazarus. The rich man lived in luxury while Lazarus suffered at his gate. When they died, the rich man went to torment while Lazarus was comforted. the patriarch Abraham explains this reversal to the tormented rich man, addressing him as "Son": "Son, remember that you, in your lifetime, received your good things, and Lazarus, in the same way, bad things. But here he is now comforted and you are in anguish" (Lk 16:25).

Of course, there are people who abuse their wealth or neglect society, but the generalization presented a startlingly simplistic binary. Rich equals bad, poor equals good. It ignored the complexity of human character.

I thought about a colleague I'd worked with in Japan. We taught together at a middle school, which was a very difficult job, if you did it properly. It didn't pay all that well, and the job comes without much social respect. He lived simply, worked hard, never displayed any signs of wealth.

Years later, when his father died and I was invited to the funeral ceremony, I discovered his family owned one of Japan's largest industrial companies. He could have lived in luxury but chose service and discipline instead.

I know poor people who are incredibly self-indulgent, and many of them are poor for this very reason. They lack discipline and foresight. And I know wealthy people who are highly disciplined and not self-indulgent at all, who use their money to support society. The Lazarus parable completely misses this reality.

Was this genuine spiritual wisdom, or populist resentment disguised as divine teaching?

Whatever his motivation, Jesus had something against money, it seems. Perhaps he had never encountered someone who used their wealth in service to others.

And I wonder how Jesus would feel knowing the Second Exodus had been hijacked and turned into the Second Empire.

But how did this happen? How could one of the most anti-empire teachers become the foundation of the most powerful empire in ancient history?

Because that's exactly what happened. Just a few hundred years after Jesus's crucifixion, Rome became Christian.

Over the subsequent centuries the Roman Catholic Church became the most influential institution the world had ever known. For over a thousand years, it controlled kings and emperors, accumulated vast wealth, and shaped entire civilizations. How did Christianity go from civilization exit to that?

Chapter 25

The Keys to the Kingdom

Throughout my investigation, I'd documented Jesus's radical teachings about human potential: we are gods who have forgotten our divine nature, capable of physical immortality if we align ourselves properly with cosmic principles.

The requirements seemed clear from scripture:

First, know your true nature: "You are gods" (Jn 10:34).

Second, purify your perception: "Judge not, so that you won't be judged" (Mt 7:1). With whatever measure you judge, it will be measured back to you. This appears to be presented as cosmic law, not mere moral advice.

Third, embrace celibacy: "Those who are considered worthy to attain to that age and the resurrection from the dead neither marry nor are given in marriage. For they can't die any more, for they are like the angels" (Lk 20:35-36).

Fourth, master the creative power of the Word: "If you have faith as a grain of mustard seed, you will tell this mountain, 'Move from here to there,' and it will move; and nothing will be impossible for you" (Mt 17:20). Your words, spoken with faith and from a pure heart, shape reality.

Fifth, live like the birds in complete trust: "Don't be anxious for your life: what you will eat, or what you will drink... See the birds of the sky, that they don't sow, neither do they reap, nor gather into barns. Your heavenly Father feeds them" (Mt 6:25-26).

Store nothing for the future. Trust divine provision absolutely. These seemed like the operational requirements for accessing our dormant immortal nature.

Practices anyone could theoretically follow if they had sufficient faith and discipline.

But there was a catch. All these practices, all this divine potential, all these radical teachings about human godhood mean nothing without one additional, non-negotiable requirement: **You must believe in Jesus as your Lord and Savior.**

He presents this claim as the absolute prerequisite for entry into the Kingdom, the one event upon which everything else depends. He reveals it in a secret, nighttime conversation with Nicodemus, a high-ranking religious scholar.

> **John 3:3-5:** *Jesus answered him, "Most certainly, I tell you, unless one is born anew, he can't see God's Kingdom." Nicodemus said to him, "How can a man be born when he is old? Can he enter a second time into his mother's womb, and be born?" Jesus answered, "Most certainly I tell you, unless one is born of water and Spirit, he can't enter into God's Kingdom."*

Nicodemus's confusion is telling. He hears this direct claim, but his literal mind cannot process it. He is a master of religious law, but this talk of a second, spiritual birth is an impossibility to him. What Jesus is presenting requires a new way of seeing.

Jesus does not leave this claim in the abstract. In his very next encounter, he provides a living, breathing demonstration of what he means. He meets a Samaritan woman at a well—an outcast, not a scholar—and in their conversation, he defines his own terms. He makes it clear that he himself is the source of this new birth.

First, he defines the "water" as a gift only he can give.

> **John 4:13-14:** *Jesus answered her, "Everyone who drinks of this water will thirst again, but whoever drinks of the **water that I will give him** will never thirst again; but the **water that I will give him** will become in him a well of water springing up to eternal life." [bolding mine]*

The claim becomes clear. The "water" of the new birth is the "living water" of eternal life that flows directly from Jesus himself.

Then, moments later, he defines the "Spirit" as the new reality this gift makes possible.

John 4:23-24: *"But the hour comes, and now is, when the true worshipers will worship the Father in **spirit and truth**, for the Father seeks such to be his worshipers. God is **spirit**, and those who worship him must worship in **spirit and truth**." [bolding mine]*

Reading these two encounters together, Jesus's claim is unmistakable. To be born again of water and Spirit is to receive the living water of eternal life *from him*, an act that transforms you by the Spirit into a new being who can relate to God directly.

This is the master key, and it is what Christians have been saying for two thousand years. It is the open secret of his entire mission: the claim that he himself is the door, the source, and the key to the Kingdom of God.

It reminds me of what he said later in the book of John to Martha just before he resurrects Lazarus: "Jesus said to her, 'I am the resurrection and the life. He who believes in me will still live, even if he dies. Whoever lives and believes in me will never die. Do you believe this?'" (Jn 11:25-26).

"Lives in" Jesus? That's an odd image, isn't it?

I couldn't see how living and believing in Jesus had anything to do with discovering your divine nature or living like the birds. I was reminded of Jesus's desire to draw all people to himself (Jn 12:32). Clearly, it's saying that believing in Jesus is the condition for immortality, isn't it?

The pattern appears throughout the Gospels:

- o "For God so loved the world, that he gave his only born Son, that whoever believes in him should not perish, but have eternal life" (Jn 3:16).
- o "Most certainly I tell you, he who believes in me has eternal life" (Jn 6:47).
- o "I am the way, the truth, and the life. No one comes to the Father, except through me" (Jn 14:6).

Clearly Jesus has positioned himself as the gatekeeper to physical immortality, requiring not only perfection of thought, feeling, and behavior, but belief in him as well. But even that is not enough. To these requirements, Jesus adds the Sermon on the Mount, filled with teachings you must follow.

The Sermon on the Mount *(Matthew 5-7, World English Bible)*

Chapter 5

Seeing the multitudes, he went up onto the mountain. When he had sat down, his disciples came to him. He opened his mouth and taught them, saying,

"Blessed are the poor in spirit, for theirs is the Kingdom of Heaven. Blessed are those who mourn, for they shall be comforted. Blessed are the gentle, for they shall inherit the earth. Blessed are those who hunger and thirst for righteousness, for they shall be filled. Blessed are the merciful, for they shall obtain mercy. Blessed are the pure in heart, for they shall see God. Blessed are the peacemakers, for they shall be called children of God. Blessed are those who have been persecuted for righteousness' sake, for theirs is the Kingdom of Heaven.

"Blessed are you when people reproach you, persecute you, and say all kinds of evil against you falsely, for my sake. Rejoice, and be exceedingly glad, for great is your reward in heaven, for so they persecuted the prophets who were before you.

"You are the salt of the earth, but if the salt has lost its flavor, with what will it be salted? It is then good for nothing, but to be cast out and trodden under the feet of men. You are the light of the world. A city located on a hill can't be hidden. Neither do you light a lamp and put it under a measuring basket, but on a stand; and it shines to all who are in the house. Even so, let your light shine before men, that they may see your good works and glorify your Father who is in heaven.

"Don't think that I came to destroy the law or the prophets. I didn't come to destroy, but to fulfill. For most certainly, I tell you, until heaven and earth pass away, not even one smallest letter or one tiny pen stroke shall in any way pass away from the law, until all things are accomplished. Therefore, whoever shall break one of these least commandments and teach others to do so, shall be called least in the Kingdom of Heaven; but whoever shall do and teach them, he shall be called great in the Kingdom of Heaven. For I tell you that unless your righteousness exceeds that of the scribes and Pharisees, you will in no way enter into the Kingdom of Heaven.

"You have heard that it was said to the ancient ones, 'You shall not murder;' and 'Whoever murders will be in danger of the judgment.' But I tell you that everyone who is angry with his brother without a cause will be in danger of the judgment. Whoever says to his brother, 'Raca!' will be in danger of the council. Whoever says, 'You fool!' will be in danger of the fire of Gehenna.

"If therefore you are offering your gift at the altar, and there remember that your brother has anything against you, leave your gift there before the altar, and go your way. First be reconciled to your brother, and then come and offer your gift. Agree with your adversary quickly while you are with him on the way; lest perhaps the prosecutor deliver you to the judge, and the judge deliver you to the officer, and you be cast into prison. Most certainly I tell you, you shall by no means get out of there until you have paid the last penny.

"You have heard that it was said, 'You shall not commit adultery;' but I tell you that everyone who gazes at a woman to lust after her has committed adultery with her already in his heart. If your right eye causes you to stumble, pluck it out and cast it from you. For it is more profitable for you that one of your members should perish than for your whole body to be cast into Gehenna. If your right hand causes you to stumble, cut it off and cast it from you. For it is more profitable for you that one of your members should perish than for your whole body to be cast into Gehenna.

Author's Note: "Gehenna" refers to the Valley of Hinnom outside Jerusalem, a place for burning garbage. Gehenna is used in Jewish thought to represent destruction or the grave, not the later Christian concept of eternal torture in hell. Regarding the instructions about removing body parts, Jesus may have meant it literally, as it seems he believed perfect physical and spiritual purity was required for immortality. However, given that his immortality teachings appear unsuccessful—no one that we know of has achieved the deathless state he promised, and even his own resurrection accounts are forensically inconsistent— I hope no one follows these harmful instructions.

"It was also said, 'Whoever shall put away his wife, let him give her a writing of divorce,' but I tell you that whoever puts away his wife, except for the cause of sexual immorality, makes her an adulteress; and whoever marries her when she is put away commits adultery.

Author's Note: *To many modern people, this teaching may seem completely unreasonable, for nearly half of our marriages end in divorce, but remember, the context matters. In first-century Palestine, divorced women faced severe economic hardship and social ostracism, with few means of independent survival. Jesus's restriction on divorce would have been understood as protecting women from arbitrary abandonment that could lead to destitution or prostitution.*

"Again you have heard that it was said to them of old time, 'You shall not make false vows, but shall perform to the Lord your vows,' but I tell you, don't swear at all: neither by heaven, for it is the throne of God; nor by the earth, for it is the footstool of his feet; nor by Jerusalem, for it is the city of the great King. Neither shall you swear by your head, for you can't make one hair white or black. But let your 'Yes' be 'Yes' and your 'No' be 'No.' Whatever is more than these is of the evil one.

"You have heard that it was said, 'An eye for an eye, and a tooth for a tooth.' But I tell you, don't resist him who is evil; but whoever strikes you on your right cheek, turn to him the other also. If anyone sues you to take away your coat, let him have your cloak also. Whoever compels you to go one mile, go with him two. Give to him who asks you, and don't turn away him who desires to borrow from you.

"You have heard that it was said, 'You shall love your neighbor and hate your enemy.' But I tell you, love your enemies, bless those who curse you, do good to those who hate you, and pray for those who mistreat you and persecute you, that you may be children of your Father who is in heaven. For he makes his sun to rise on the evil and the good, and sends rain on the just and the unjust. For if you love those who love you, what reward do you have? Don't even the tax collectors do the same? If you only greet your friends, what more do you do than others? Don't even the tax collectors do the same? Therefore you shall be perfect, just as your Father in heaven is perfect.

Chapter 6

"Be careful that you don't do your charitable giving before men, to be seen by them, or else you have no reward from your Father who is in heaven. Therefore, when you do merciful deeds, don't sound a trumpet before yourself, as the hypocrites do in the synagogues and in the streets, that they may get glory from men. Most certainly I tell you, they have received their reward. But when you do merciful deeds, don't let your left hand know what your right hand does, so that your merciful deeds may be in secret, then your Father who sees in secret will reward you openly.

"When you pray, you shall not be as the hypocrites, for they love to stand and pray in the synagogues and in the corners of the streets, that they may be seen by men. Most certainly I tell you, they have received their reward. But you, when you pray, enter into your inner room, and having shut your door, pray to your Father who is in secret; and your Father who sees in secret will reward you openly. In praying, don't use vain repetitions as the Gentiles do, for they think that they will be heard for their much speaking. Therefore don't be like them, for your Father knows what things you need before you ask him.

"Pray like this: 'Our Father in heaven, may your name be kept holy. Let your Kingdom come. Let your will be done on earth as it is in heaven. Give us today our daily bread. Forgive us our debts, as we also forgive our debtors. Bring us not into temptation, but deliver us from the evil one. For yours is the Kingdom, the power, and the glory forever. Amen.'

Author's Note: *The phrase "deliver us from the evil one" comes from the Greek* tou ponērou, *which could mean either "the evil one" (a judgmental label directed at the Devil) or simply "evil" (as an abstract concept). The World English Bible uses "the evil one," as do many modern translations, but that may not have been what Jesus meant.*

"For if you forgive men their trespasses, your heavenly Father will also forgive you. But if you don't forgive men their trespasses, neither will your Father forgive your trespasses.

"Moreover when you fast, don't be like the hypocrites, with sad faces. For they disfigure their faces that they may be seen by men to be fasting. Most certainly I tell you, they have received their reward. But you, when you fast, anoint your head and wash your face, so that you are not seen by men to be fasting, but by your Father who is in secret; and your Father who sees in secret will reward you openly.

"Don't lay up treasures for yourselves on the earth, where moth and rust consume, and where thieves break through and steal; but lay up for yourselves treasures in heaven, where neither moth nor rust consume, and where thieves don't break through and steal; for where your treasure is, there your heart will be also.

"The lamp of the body is the eye. If therefore your eye is sound, your whole body will be full of light. But if your eye is evil, your whole body will be full of darkness. If therefore the light that is in you is darkness, how great is the darkness!

Author's Note: "*If your eye is evil*" *translates an idiom that Jesus's audience would have immediately understood. In Jewish and Mediterranean culture, an "evil eye" meant stinginess, envy, or a grudging disposition, while a "good eye" meant generosity. Jesus was using figurative language about vision and light to teach about how one's internal attitude—generous versus stingy—affects one's entire spiritual state. He was not judging people as evil here, but using a common metaphor about perspective and character.*

"No one can serve two masters, for either he will hate the one and love the other, or else he will be devoted to one and despise the other. You can't serve both God and Mammon.

"Therefore I tell you, don't be anxious for your life: what you will eat, or what you will drink; nor yet for your body, what you will wear. Isn't life more than food, and the body more than clothing? See the birds of the sky, that they don't sow, neither do they reap, nor gather into barns. Your heavenly Father feeds them. Aren't you of much more value than they?

"Which of you by being anxious, can add one moment to his lifespan? Why are you anxious about clothing? Consider the lilies of the field, how they grow. They don't toil, neither do they spin, yet I tell you that even Solomon in all his glory was not dressed like one of these. But if God so clothes the grass of the field, which today exists and tomorrow is thrown into the oven, won't he much more clothe you, you of little faith?

"Therefore don't be anxious, saying, 'What will we eat?', 'What will we drink?' or, 'With what will we be clothed?' For the Gentiles seek after all these things; for your heavenly Father knows that you need all these things. But seek first God's Kingdom and his righteousness; and all these things will be given to you as well. Therefore don't be anxious for tomorrow, for tomorrow will be anxious for itself. Each day's own evil is sufficient.

Author's Note: The phrase "each day's own evil" translates the Greek kakia, which can mean evil/wickedness (a moral judgment) or simply trouble/difficulty (a neutral description). Many translations use "evil," but "trouble" would be equally valid: "Each day has enough trouble of its own." This changes the passage from sounding like a judgment about the moral nature of daily existence to practical wisdom about not adding tomorrow's worries to today's challenges.

Chapter 7

"Don't judge, so that you won't be judged. For with whatever judgment you judge, you will be judged; and with whatever measure you measure, it will be measured to you. Why do you see the speck that is in your brother's eye, but don't consider the beam that is in your own eye? Or how will you tell your brother, 'Let me remove the speck from your eye,' and behold, the beam is in your own eye? You hypocrite! First remove the beam out of your own eye, and then you can see clearly to remove the speck out of your brother's eye.

Author's Note: Within the very paragraph where he admonishes the crowd not to judge, he judges. Many more judgments are to follow. See if you can spot them as you observe his teachings.

"Don't give that which is holy to the dogs, neither throw your pearls before the pigs, lest perhaps they trample them under their feet, and turn and tear you.

"Ask, and it will be given you. Seek, and you will find. Knock, and it will be opened for you. For everyone who asks receives. He who seeks finds. To him who knocks it will be opened. Or who is there among you who, if his son asks him for bread, will give him a stone? Or if he asks for a fish, who will give him a serpent? If you then, being evil, know how to give good gifts to your children, how much more will your Father who is in heaven give good things to those who ask him?

"Therefore, whatever you desire for men to do to you, you shall also do to them; for this is the law and the prophets.

"Enter in by the narrow gate; for the gate is wide and the way is broad that leads to destruction, and there are many who enter in by it. How narrow is the gate and restricted is the way that leads to life! There are few who find it.

"Beware of false prophets, who come to you in sheep's clothing, but inwardly are ravening wolves. By their fruits you will know them. Do men gather grapes from thorns or figs from thistles? Even so, every good tree produces good fruit, but the corrupt tree produces evil fruit. A good tree can't produce evil fruit, neither can a corrupt tree produce good fruit. Every tree that doesn't grow good fruit is cut down and thrown into the fire. Therefore by their fruits you will know them.

"Not everyone who says to me, 'Lord, Lord,' will enter into the Kingdom of Heaven, but he who does the will of my Father who is in heaven. Many will tell me in that day, 'Lord, Lord, didn't we prophesy in your name, in your name cast out demons, and in your name do many mighty works?' Then I will tell them, 'I never knew you. Depart from me, you who work iniquity.'

Author's Note: *There it is. Jesus claims to be the ultimate decider.*

"Everyone therefore who hears these words of mine and does them, I will liken him to a wise man who built his house on a rock. The rain came down, the floods came, and the winds blew and beat on that house; and it didn't fall, for it was founded on a rock. Everyone who hears these words of mine and doesn't do them will be like a foolish man who built his house on the sand. The rain came down, the floods came, and the winds blew and beat on that house; and it fell—and its fall was great."

When Jesus had finished saying these things, the multitudes were astonished at his teaching, for he taught them with authority, and not like the scribes.

Here we find a Jesus who stressed living with integrity, loving unconditionally, and maintaining direct relationship with the divine, but with a catch—*through him.*

And this is where the Jews largely rejected Jesus and his teachings. The reasoning becomes clearer when we understand what "Messiah" meant to first-century Jews.

Unlike later Christian theology, Jews didn't expect the Messiah to be God incarnate demanding worship. The Messiah was understood as God's anointed servant—a descendant of King David who would serve divine purposes to restore Israel's independence from Roman occupation and reestablish God's kingdom on earth.

The Messiah was supposed to be God's agent, not God's equal. He was an anointed king who would point people toward God, not toward himself. He was to liberate through divine authority, not extract worship through divine claims.

Jesus changed the messianic role into something Jews never expected: a demand for worship as God's equal rather than service as God's appointed. His "follow me" meant "worship me as the exclusive gateway to salvation."

This, in part, explains why the Jews rejected Jesus's claims. For Christians, it helps to know that "Christ" is the Greek translation of "Messiah," and thus, it means "servant." To the Jews, a servant is not equal to his master, and thus Christ is not God's equal.

The Messiah would be a political king, who would fight for the laws of God and liberate them from Roman control, and restore the temple. As Jesus did not liberate the Jews and restore the temple, neither version of Jesus could be the Messiah in their eyes.

It's true that many Jews followed Jesus initially, probably expecting him to use his demonstrated miraculous power to overthrow Roman occupation supernaturally. They probably imagined him casting down lightning bolts like God did to Sodom and Gomorrah. The palm branches they waved when Jesus entered Jerusalem on a donkey were symbols of victory and liberation.

However, Jesus's claims to divine equality created a theological crisis that no amount of miraculous power could resolve. Jews could accept a powerful Messiah who served God, but not one who positioned himself as God's equal.

This explains why disciples couldn't accept Jesus's predictions of crucifixion despite hearing them repeatedly. They expected divine intervention against Rome, not a shameful, suffering death that indicates separation from God. When political liberation didn't materialize and claims of Jesus's divinity became central, many Jewish followers abandoned the movement.

Ultimately, Jesus did not deliver what Jews understood the Messiah was supposed to accomplish—concrete liberation from Roman occupation and restoration of Jewish sovereignty.

Part IV

Beyond Jesus

In Part III, we stepped away from the unsettling patterns of the character to excavate his words. We unearthed a set of teachings so radical and profound—about our own divinity, about unconditional love, about physical immortality—that they felt like they could be the very "bones" we were searching for. Now, we stand at the heart of the paradox.

How can these seemingly pure, liberating teachings coexist with the disturbing actions of the man we met in Part I? Is it possible that we have found two different Jesuses woven into a single narrative—one the sublime teacher, the other a sinister manipulator?

I know how tempting it is to believe so. My own heart desperately wanted to cling to this hope—to save a "Good Jesus" from the wreckage of the "Bad Jesus." This is the most powerful impulse we've faced yet: the desire to believe we have finally found the clean, authentic truth we've been searching for.

But our discipline as detectives demands that we treat this, too, as a clue, not a conclusion. We must resist the urge to create a comfortable story.

So, in Part IV, "Beyond Jesus," we will step back from the character and his teachings to examine the immense and contradictory legacy he left behind. Our investigation now moves from the text to the world, from the man to the movement he inspired. We will follow the trail of evidence and ask: How did a radical, anti-empire teaching become the foundation for the most powerful empire on earth? Who was Paul, and did he corrupt the beautiful message we just uncovered, or was he completing a plan we have not yet fully understood?

This is where the final pieces of the puzzle begin to snap into place.

Chapter 26

The Great Inversion

As I sat with these radical teachings about divine love and civilization exit, I couldn't escape the contradictions that had brought me here. How could the same person who taught us of our own godhood simultaneously behave with such a focus on his own glory?

Had the narratives been manipulated? What if scripture no longer reflects much of what Jesus taught, as the Jesus in my childhood dreams suggested? This led me to investigate the man who perhaps shaped Christianity more than anyone else: Paul.

As I read Paul's epistles, an aversion I'd felt since childhood began stirring. It was that same uneasy feeling I'd never been able to put my finger on.

I'd never understood where this aversion came from. But thinking about it now, I remembered something important about my childhood relationship with scripture.

When I was a child, I was functionally illiterate. I did not really learn how to read until I was sixteen. My reading comprehension was so poor that I had to read and reread anything to digest it.

But I was determined to read the Bible. I started with Matthew because it was the first Gospel. I think I may have only gotten through the Sermon on the Mount initially, but I read it over and over, working hard to understand every word.

Those teachings became my spiritual foundation: the vision of living like the birds and lilies, trusting in divine provision, free from anxiety about survival.

"Consider the lilies of the field, how they grow: They don't toil, neither do they spin, yet I tell you that even Solomon in all his glory was not arrayed like one of these" (Mt 6:28).

I found this beautiful. It felt like we could live independently again in Eden, at one with nature and the animals. At one with God.

Years later, when I heard Paul's teachings in church, something felt wrong. His teachings seemed at odds with what I'd absorbed from the Sermon on the Mount. But I couldn't articulate why.

Now, decades later, I found myself wondering if Paul had somehow corrupted Jesus's authentic teachings. I looked up the estimated dates of all New Testament scripture, and I was stunned to learn that Paul's epistles are *older* than the four Gospel accounts of Jesus!

Paul was writing his institutional salvation theology at around 70 CE (three to four decades after Jesus's crucifixion), while the Gospel narratives were written decades later, between 80 and 100 CE.

When the Gospel writers sat down to compose Jesus's life story, Paul's letters had been circulating everywhere for decades. What if Paul's *Lord Jesus Christ* formula was already the established theology in many Christian communities?

My mind wanted to exonerate Jesus by putting what I saw as corrupted teachings on Paul, but then I stumbled across something that likely most Christians already know.

According to the Book of Acts and Paul's letters, he didn't work in isolation from Jesus's disciples. If his writings and the church records are to be believed, he'd collaborated with Peter and John—Jesus's closest companions—and with Jesus's brother James for years.

How did Paul's systematic inversions of Jesus's second Exodus teachings gain such widespread acceptance? The answer may lie in a combination of factors: the apostles' own disillusionment after Jesus's failed promises of physical resurrection—a failure suggested by the fact that none of the Gospel accounts align, ranging from Mark's original silence to Matthew's zombie apocalypse—the practical impossibility of living by the Sermon on the Mount teachings, and the appeal of a more socially integrated form of Christianity that didn't require total civilization exit.

145

Whatever the precise dynamics, the result was clear: within decades of Jesus's death, the radical path of living like birds and trusting divine provision had been replaced by institutional Christianity with property, hierarchy, and integration with existing social structures.

And then I discovered something else I had not known. According to Paul, Peter, James, and John had actively partnered with him to establish churches throughout the region.

I preferred to think Paul had fabricated his collaboration with the disciples. Or that Peter, James, and John, like Judas had betrayed Jesus, once they realized he did not resurrect, as he had promised.

But wanting something to be so does not make it so. I had to accept the possibility that Jesus wasn't the man I wanted him to be.

According to church tradition, James led the Jerusalem church. Peter was associated with founding the church in Rome; John with the church in Ephesus.

The church structure appears to be somewhere between total property abandonment and conventional church structure. Acts 2:44-47 describes believers having "all things in common" and selling possessions to distribute to those in need:

> *44 All who believed were together, and had all things in common. 45 They sold their possessions and goods, and distributed them to all, according as anyone had need. 46 Day by day, continuing steadfastly with one accord in the temple, and breaking bread at home, they took their food with gladness and singleness of heart, 47 praising God and having favor with all the people. The Lord added to the assembly day by day those who were being saved.*

Acts 4:32-37 shows continued property sharing in the Jerusalem community:

> *32 The multitude of those who believed were of one heart and soul. Neither did anyone say that any of the things which he possessed was his own, but they had all things in common. 33 With great power, the apostles gave their testimony of the resurrection of the Lord Jesus. Great grace was on them all. 34 For neither was there among them anyone who lacked, for as many as were owners of lands or houses sold them, and brought the proceeds of the things that were sold, 35 and laid them at the apostles' feet. Then distribution was made to each,*

according as anyone had need. 36 Joseph, who by the apostles was surnamed Barnabas (which is, being interpreted, Son of Encouragement), a Levite, a man of Cyprus by birth, 37 having a field, sold it, and brought the money and laid it at the apostles' feet.

They sound like communes, don't they? Most modern Christians reject communes entirely, it seems. How'd that happen?

What happened to the teachings that we are physically immortal? And what happened to the teachings of a totally just universe where you reap what you sow? What happened to the power of the Word? What happened to independence from organizations?

It seems the entire focus had become exclusively about believing Jesus was God, which, at least to me, feels like ego worship. I think it's fair to say that we would feel that way if any other human or deity said such things. Why were Peter, James, and John working with Paul teaching things that seemed to contradict the Sermon on the Mount?

Let's follow this trail.

I started comparing what seemed like two completely different spiritual paths found in the Gospels.

When I looked at the Sermon on the Mount, I saw what appeared to be a radical civilization-exit strategy: sell everything we have, live as if we are immortal gods, not marrying, not thinking of the future, not resisting evil, but with Jesus as God's gatekeeper.

But Paul's letters seemed to teach something quite different. From my perspective, in them, most of the principles from the Sermon on the Mount had been systematically inverted. Where Jesus appeared to teach complete independence from all systems, Paul taught integration with family, government, and religious institutions.

But was I seeing patterns that weren't really there? I decided to check systematically. Here are a few core inversions from Jesus's radical teachings.

Jesus: Sell everything you have and give to the poor. Don't store up treasures on earth. Don't marry.

Paul: Support family structures. Provide for your household. Build institutions with property and wealth.

Jesus: You are gods. Be perfect as your Father in heaven is perfect.

Paul: You are wretched and need salvation through institutional belief in Jesus.

Jesus: Complete civilization exit—live like the birds, trust divine provision.

Paul: Remain in your assigned place in society. Integrate with governmental and social structures.

Jesus: Direct relationship with God as children and co-heirs—"you are gods" (Jn 10:34).

Paul: You are purchased property—"You are not your own, for you were bought with a price. Therefore glorify God in your body and in your spirit, which are God's." (1 Cor 6:19-20).

Bought at a price. Think about this—who buys souls? Possession replacing divine sonship.

The pattern was so consistent it took my breath away. Every radical independence teaching had been turned into its opposite, creating dependency on exactly the systems Jesus seemed to be calling people out of.

What do you think? Was this accidental, or was something more systematic at work? The pattern was so consistent that I began wondering if Paul had intentionally inverted the radical practices Jesus taught.

Paul's letter to the Romans contains the most astonishing inversion of all: "The law came in that the trespass might abound; but where sin abounded, grace abounded more exceedingly" (Rom 5:20).

Wait. Was Paul really saying that God gave the Law specifically to *increase* sin?

I thought about how even toddlers know unfairness instinctively. Give one child more than another, and the shorted one loses their mind. Same with chimps in experiments—give one a grape and another a cucumber for the same task, and the cucumber chimp goes ballistic.

No one taught them about fairness. They just *know.*

So where was Paul getting this idea that we can't recognize sin without explicit rules? And if the Law was designed to increase sin, and Jesus came to fulfill the Law, wasn't Paul saying Jesus came to make things *worse?*

The Great Inversion

The more I read, the darker it got. In Romans 9, Paul seemed to be describing a God who appears to operate from a place of cosmic self-interest: "For the Scripture says to Pharaoh, 'For this very purpose I caused you to be raised up, that I might show in you my power, and that my name might be proclaimed in all the earth.' So then he has mercy on whom he desires, and he hardens whom he desires."

I traced this back to its source in Exodus 9:16, where "the Lord" tells Pharaoh through Moses the same thing. I slowly reread the passage, trying to process it.

Paul was saying that God admits to creating Pharaoh specifically to destroy him as a demonstration of divine power. Not because Pharaoh chose evil, but because God needed a villain for his cosmic theater.

It's a dark thought, but it's backed by scripture.

Paul continued this logic: "What if God, willing to show his wrath and to make his power known, endured with much patience vessels of wrath fitted for destruction, that he might make known the riches of his glory on vessels of mercy, which he prepared beforehand for glory" (Rom 9:22).

According to Paul's theory, God intentionally creates "vessels of wrath fitted for destruction"—people specifically designed to cause harm and be damned—just to make his mercy toward others look more impressive by contrast.

Wasn't Paul suggesting that God creates the problem, then offers himself as the solution while demanding gratitude for his "mercy"?

It's like a firefighter secretly setting houses ablaze so he can be the hero who puts out the fires. The same entity creating the crisis then expects worship for providing the rescue.

Maximum worship extraction through manufactured crisis and salvation. This is the signature of the Cosmic Ego.

And that brings us back to the figure of Lucifer, who appears to have been created with the specific aim to corrupt humanity, setting the stage for a glorious rescue.

If my earlier analysis was correct—that the "Lord God" speaking throughout much of the Old Testament was actually Lucifer impersonating YHWH—then

Paul was quoting Lucifer's own admission of his manipulative tactics as proof of divine righteousness.

In essence, it seems Paul was saying: "What if God creates people just to torture them for his own glorification, and we should worship him for this!"

Whether it was the true YHWH or the imposter speaking in Exodus, the character being described displayed every trait modern psychology associates with narcissism, Machiavellianism, sadism, and psychopathy: creating suffering for personal glory, manipulating people like puppets, then punishing them for the very behaviors that were programmed into them.

It was a sickening realization. If Paul's theology was accurate, then Judaism, Christianity, and Islam—with their combined four billion followers—were all worshipping a being who creates beings specifically to damn them.

Maybe we aren't looking at different religions, so much as looking at the same deceptive spirit wearing different masks.

I so wish there were another way to read this without lying to myself, but I just can't see it without resorting to the mind-bending twists of apologetics. Can you?

As if to cement his authority, Paul goes further in his letter to the Galatians, cursing in God's name anyone who dares teach a different version of the Gospel:

"I am astonished that you are so quickly deserting the one who called you to live in the grace of Christ and are turning to a different gospel—which is really no gospel at all. Evidently some people are throwing you into confusion and are trying to pervert the gospel of Christ. But even if we or an angel from heaven should preach a gospel other than the one we preached to you, let them be under God's curse!" (Galatians 1:6-9).

Even if an angel from heaven? Angels are considered God's direct messengers. Hubris?

It raises the question: If the message is truly liberating, why be so defensive about it? What happened to love your enemies and turn the other cheek? Where is the grace here?

Chapter 27

The Mind Trap

How had Paul managed to make these inversions invisible to believers for two thousand years? The answer may lay in the psychological mechanisms he'd embedded in his theology.

Maybe Paul's warning in 2 Corinthians 11:14–15: "No wonder, for even Satan masquerades as an angel of light. Therefore it is no great thing if his servants also masquerade as servants of righteousness, whose end will be according to their works" provided the answer.

Could Paul have been subconsciously revealing the very strategy he was employing? Or was he unconsciously revealing something about Jesus?

That childhood unease was beginning to make sense to me. It seemed to me that Paul was systematically demonizing our natural capacity to detect contradictions as a spiritual failing.

Paul made this explicit in 1 Corinthians 1:18: "For the message of the cross is foolishness to those who are perishing, but to us who are being saved it is the power of God... For the foolishness of God is wiser than men, and the weakness of God is stronger than men."

And then came the kicker: "Let no one deceive himself. If anyone thinks that he is wise among you in this world, let him become a fool, that he may become wise. For the wisdom of this world is foolishness with God" (1 Cor 3:18).

Become a fool to become wise? I had always assumed Paul was saying something similar to Socrates, who said "Know that you know nothing," which is quite wise.

But reading the full range of Paul's teachings, I felt he wasn't suggesting we be humble like Socrates, who knew that he knew nothing but still maintained sharp critical thinking. It appears Paul was saying something far more dangerous: *If something in Christianity doesn't make logical sense, don't trust your reasoning. Trust the message anyway.*

The psychological manipulation is staggering. Any time someone points out inconsistencies, theological contradictions, or ethical problems, the response is automatic: "You're relying on worldly wisdom, but God's ways are higher than our ways." "It's not for us to question God."

I thought back to my own experiences in Bible study. Those moments when I'd ask honest questions about obvious contradictions, only to be met with gentle dismissals or word-salad explanations that made no sense. The subtle message was always the same: *questioning itself was the problem, not the contradictions.*

How many of us learned to suppress our natural sense of fairness and logic to avoid that uncomfortable feeling of challenging what everyone else accepted? How many children have been trained to doubt their own perception when it conflicts with religious authority?

Paul had created near-perfect immunity against critical examination. Once someone accepted that their reasoning was "worldly" and "foolish," they became defenseless against any claim made in God's name.

The pattern was breathtaking in its completeness. Paul had attracted and created followers who'd been trained to dismiss their own capacity for discernment in favor of unquestioning submission. And he'd disguised this psychological conditioning as spiritual wisdom. This is exactly how cults work, is it not?

Those teachings demand total mental occupation: "Take every thought captive to Christ" (2 Cor 10:5). Complete psychological possession.

This brings us back to Ego. What is more egoic than demanding the total surrender of independent thought?

Chapter 28

Lingering Questions

After documenting the big picture of the New Testament, I still had some lingering questions. You may have wondered about some of these passages yourself. Let's see if we can answer them.

The first unresolved puzzle arose from passages where Jesus refers to mysterious enemies: "the prince of this world" and what Paul calls "the god of this age." But Jesus couldn't be any less clear about what he means.

"Now is the judgment of this world. Now *the prince of this world* will be cast out" (Jn 12:31). [emphasis mine]

"I will no more speak much with you, for *the prince of the world* comes, and he has nothing in me" (Jn 14:30).

"In whom *the god of this world* has blinded the minds of the unbelieving, that the light of the Good News of the glory of Christ, who is the image of God, should not dawn on them" (2 Cor 4:4).

Wait. Who is this? Is he talking about Lucifer or Satan—or maybe some other nefarious being? The vague references left me wondering if I'd missed something crucial.

After much research, I found that Jesus never directly explains what he means by these titles, so what I'm about to share is speculation based on the big picture of his ministry.

I started asking myself: Who were Jesus's actual enemies throughout the Gospels? Who consistently opposed him? Wasn't it people asking reasonable questions? People demanding evidence? People thinking critically about his claims?

The Pharisees asking for proof of his authority? Jesus calls them "evil" and "faithless." His own family thinking he might be mentally unwell based on his behavior? He disowns them. He repeatedly laments anyone who questions his contradictory teachings or fails to follow through on seemingly irrational commands.

Then I remembered the key passage in Mark 4:15, where Jesus explains his parable of the sower: "The ones by the road are the ones where the word is sown; and when they have heard, immediately Satan comes and takes away the word which has been sown in them."

But what actually "takes away" belief in Jesus's teachings? What makes people stop believing once they've heard his message? Isn't it critical thinking? Logical analysis? Evidence-based reasoning? The very mental faculties that would expose the contradictions and seeming hypocrisies that are throughout the New Testament?

Here's my theory: likely, gospel writers or later scribes redefined Satan, not just as the enemy of humanity, as is stated in the Old Testament, but also as critical thinking—the force that removes belief from people's minds through rational evaluation.

Think about it. Jesus consistently demanded blind faith over evidence. "Blessed are those who believe without seeing." And he often judged those who asked seemingly reasonable questions. From this pattern, he seems to have made critical thinking itself into a sin.

During my research for my previous book *The Genesis Code*, I found that in ancient cultures, abstract concepts like wisdom, logic, and reasoning were routinely connected to gods and spirits.

For example, Paul refers to Satan as "the prince of the power of the air" (Eph 2:2)—the space between the material world and the divine. This "air" realm could represent the domain of thought and reasoning, the mental space where we evaluate and judge claims.

Did Gospel writers identify logic and reason themselves as "the prince of this world" and "the god of this age"?

Here's my theory: what if gospel writers redefined the adversary not just as the enemy of humanity, but as critical thinking itself. If so, it would explain a lot. The primary threat to a narrative full of contradictions is a mind that notices them. Wouldn't the system, therefore, have to frame critical thinking as the enemy?

But Jesus mentioned another entity that he largely left undefined. He promised his followers another helper: "I will pray to the Father, and he will give you another Counselor, that he may be with you forever: the Spirit of truth, whom the world can't receive, for it doesn't see him and doesn't know him. You know him, for he lives with you and will be in you" (Jn 14:16–17).

The Spirit of truth? We talked about the Holy Spirit in relation to eternal punishment in Chapter 19. Is the Spirit of truth equal to the Holy Spirit? Let's look at the Spirit of truth from another angle to see what we find.

What is truth? And what did this "Spirit of truth" actually produce? Blind belief regardless of evidence? A total inversion of truth, where facts don't matter—only what you're told to believe about what the Bible says?

Is truth opposed to evidence, logical consistency, and honest evaluation? It seems the Gospel writer's idea of truth demands the abandonment of all these faculties.

Believe in me absolutely and damn all evidence to the contrary—isn't that exactly what the Cosmic Ego would say?

In the narrative, Jesus starts with incredible spiritual gifts, gathers followers, then he systematically conditions them away from critical thinking toward absolute devotion.

Isn't this classic cult behavior? Making questioning itself into betrayal?

The pattern extends far beyond religious movements. We see it in corrupt governments, manipulative influencers, dishonest advertisers, various ideologies, and anyone who demands unquestioning belief while attacking the very mental faculties that would expose their deception.

This pattern succeeds because it exploits our deepest desires for belonging while disarming our protective instincts. We want meaning, purpose, connection to something greater and to community.

It seems to me that when we surrender our discernment to get this kind of organizational belonging or identity, we become vulnerable to exactly the kind of manipulation that destroys lives.

Haven't you seen the dangers of blind belief in your own life or in the lives of loved ones?

As I think about my childhood experiences in Bible Study and Sunday school, asking questions and being shut down or being fed a pastoral word-salad, I see that a seed was planted, but not one of the church.

Sometimes a child's simple questions—"But that doesn't make sense," "Why can't I ask that?"—can tear down all the artifice, if the child sticks to their guns.

Over the years, I've heard so many pastors say that the beauty of Christianity is that it is coherent, but I've found the opposite to be true. For example, when I examined the timeline of Satan's expulsions, I felt baffled. The biblical narrative presents what appears to be multiple banishments of the same entity.

In Genesis 3, the serpent is cursed and expelled from Eden along with Adam and Eve. But in the Book of Revelation, we find Satan being cast out of heaven during a cosmic war: "And there was war in heaven: Michael and his angels fought against the dragon; and the dragon fought and his angels... And the great dragon was cast out, that old serpent, called the Devil, and Satan" (Rev 12:7-9).

How could Satan be expelled from paradise twice?—once from "Eden" (Genesis 3) and again in the Book of Revelation. When did this second expulsion occur? Before creation? After the fall? During Jesus's ministry? The Book of Revelation seems to present it as happening as a result of Jesus ascending to the throne in Eden after his resurrection.

The timeline of Satan's expulsions is a baffling contradiction. Adding to the confusion is the separate figure of Lucifer. Lucifer's fall, described in Isaiah (Old Testament) happened well before Jesus's time—"How you have fallen from heaven, morning star, son of the dawn!" That adds another layer of confusion. Two falls of Satan and a fall of Lucifer?

And when Jesus, Lucifer's Messiah rose, is that Lucifer rising yet again to heaven? Was YHWH unable to see through the ruse as he sat next to Jesus on the throne in Eden?

The biblical narrative provides no reconciliation. We're left with these fundamental questions: If Satan was already expelled from Eden, how was he later in heaven to be cast out again? If Lucifer had been banished by YHWH, why was he allowed back into heaven through Jesus?

Even if we deny the Jesus is Lucifer's Messiah theory, we're still stuck with the question of why Jesus would need to throw the serpent out of Eden, when he was already cast out.

These theological inconsistencies illustrate the logical problems that emerge when trying to read scripture as a unified, coherent narrative. Rather than resolving into clarity, the contradictions multiply the more carefully we examine them.

Another point of confusion is the question of evil. Throughout the Gospels, Jesus speaks of "testifying to the evil of this world" and judges various people and systems as evil. But on what basis does he make these moral pronouncements, when his own moral consistency is lacking? How does Jesus define good and evil?

My first assumption was based on a common Christian idea of good and evil. It goes like this: "Good is what God loves, and evil is what God hates." From that idea, I could refer to the Old Testament to see what God loves and hates, based on what he does.

I was horrified by what I found. Here is but one example of many—YHWH's commands regarding the city of Jericho from Joshua 6:17-21:

"The city shall be devoted, even it and all that is in it, to Yahweh. Only Rahab the prostitute shall live, she and all who are with her in the house, because she hid the messengers that we sent. But as for you, only keep yourselves from what is devoted to destruction, lest when you have devoted it, you take of the devoted thing and make the camp of Israel accursed and trouble it. But all the silver, gold, and vessels of bronze and iron are holy to Yahweh. They shall come into Yahweh's treasury."

Author's Note: *The Hebrew word translated as "devoted" is* "herem," *which means devoted to destruction or placed under a ban. This was a religious concept where everything in a conquered city was to be destroyed as an offering to YHWH.*

The account continues: "So the people shouted and the priests blew the trumpets. When the people heard the sound of the trumpet, the people shouted with a great shout, and the wall fell down flat, so that the people went up into the city, every man straight before him, and they took the city. They completely destroyed all that was in the city, both man and woman, both young and old, and ox, sheep, and donkey, with the edge of the sword."

The command is said to come directly from YHWH through Joshua, making it a divinely ordered genocide according to the biblical text. Christian thinking necessarily equates this genocide as good.

But Jesus said to love your enemy, turn the other cheek, and not to use the sword. Clearly, Jesus differed from the prophets of the past in his view of God. So, does Jesus's command mean that God's genocidal order was evil?

I was even more confused when Jesus said he came to fulfill the prophets to the last word, but the prophets he would be fulfilling include Joshua, who conveyed God's order of genocide.

Part of my confusion stems from the incredible inconsistencies in the Gospels. Trying to track Jesus's logic is bewildering, and that makes tracking his definitions of good and evil difficult.

Another pattern troubled me: the prophecies Jesus claimed proved his identity didn't seem to refer to him at all.

Christianity stakes everything on Jesus being the prophesied Messiah. But when I traced the Old Testament passages back to their original context, I found something disturbing: these don't seem to be, in any way, prophecies about a future messiah—they were about contemporary events in ancient Israel.

Take Isaiah 7:14, the famous "virgin birth" prophecy. In context, Isaiah is giving King Ahaz a sign about an immediate political crisis: a young woman (Hebrew: *almah*, meaning young woman, not virgin) would conceive, and before the child grew up, the threatening kingdoms would fall. This was about 8th century BC Assyrian politics, not a messiah 700 years later.

The "virgin" reading only exists because the Greek Septuagint mistranslated *almah* as *parthenos* (virgin). The entire virgin birth doctrine rests on a translation error.

Or Hosea 11:1: "Out of Egypt I called my son." Matthew claims this prophesies Jesus's return from Egypt as an infant. But read Hosea—it's explicitly about God calling *Israel* out of Egyptian slavery during the Exodus. It's not prophecy; it's history.

The pattern was consistent. Passages ripped from context, mistranslated, or completely reinterpreted to manufacture proof of Jesus's divine identity.

Was this deliberate deception? Genuine belief in connections that weren't there? Or evidence that the Gospel writers were constructing a theological narrative rather than recording history?

Whatever the answer, it revealed how desperately the early church needed to establish Jesus's credentials—even if that meant twisting scripture to do it.

And that brings me to questions I personally have about how we could have been so wrong about Jesus for so long.

Regarding the egoic face of Jesus, the disguise seems so thin now, like the glasses Clark Kent used to hide his alter ego, Superman.

But Christians can't see it.

When I share the findings of this book with devout fundamentalist Christians, they are unwilling to admit that Jesus represents Lucifer, despite Jesus describing himself as such.

But what I found even more baffling was that they don't consider Lucifer evil because he's egotistical. Ego is not the problem, per se. They point out that God condemned Lucifer for refusing to submit to God's hierarchy.

While traditional theology identifies the first sin as disobedience, the Genesis narrative shows the motivation was the desire to "be like God"—the same prideful ambition attributed to Lucifer's fall.

This is where it gets confusing. Jesus too, according to scripture, aimed for equality with God. We can see that played out in Revelation when the lamb ascends to the throne in Eden next to God.

But it gets still more confusing. Christianity means to be "Christ-like." The very name of the religion suggests that we are supposed to be equal to Christ. But isn't that desire evil?

If Christ is God, then logically Christians must emulate the behaviors they attribute to God—including demanding worship, seeking glory, and threatening punishment for disobedience.

Yet Christians simultaneously condemn these same behaviors as sinful pride when displayed by humans, creating an impossible ethical framework where believers are called to be like Christ while being forbidden from acting like Christ.

Even when I point out these contradictions, they claim not to see a problem.

From these experiences, I began wondering what it is to be Christian. As best as I can tell, a Christian believes that whatever God does is good, even if they would consider those same behaviors evil if a human being did them of their own will.

If God demands glorification, it's good.
If God commands genocide, it's good.
If God judges you to eternal torment for not believing in him, it is good.

It seems the question my father asked when I was eight years old cuts through all the theological complexity:

"Would you love and respect a God that would send people to Hell for eternity just for being of a different religion?"

A committed Christian must answer "Yes."

There is no reasoning with that mindset, is there?

Chapter 29

The Imperial Gospel

Now that I saw what a straightforward reading of the Bible revealed, I simply could not fathom how Christianity became the dominant religion of the world. Of all the Messiah's "miracles," two billion people calling themselves Christian might be the greatest! How?

Buddhism had beautiful teachings. So did Taoism. Judaism had ancient wisdom. Yet Christianity spread across the globe in ways these other religions never matched. And it did so not through superior philosophy, or even coherent teachings, but through something else.

What was that?

I thought about the gentle souls Jesus seemed to be calling—the ones who couldn't make it in aggressive systems, the "poor in spirit," the meek. Jesus offered them an exit strategy from civilization itself.

But that's not what spread across the world.

What spread was churches, institutions, hierarchies. Christian empires conquering continents. For centuries, the most powerful nations on earth flew Christian flags.

That's not the pattern you'd expect from "sell everything, live like the birds, call no man master."

Then I came across Romans 13:1-7: "Let every soul be in subjection to the higher authorities, for there is no authority except from God, and those who exist are ordained by God. Therefore he who resists the authority withstands the ordinance of God; and those who withstand will receive to themselves judgment."

I had found my answer. Paul was saying that political authority comes from God. That resisting government is resisting God. That obedience to earthly rulers is spiritual obedience.

Couldn't this psychological conditioning empower any authority figure?

"Servants, be obedient to those who according to the flesh are your masters, with fear and trembling, in singleness of your heart, as to Christ" (Eph 6:5).

"Wives, be subject to your own husbands, as to the Lord" (Eph 5:22).

Paul had systematically woven Christianity into every hierarchical structure: government, slavery, family. And in each case, he'd made obedience to earthly authority equivalent to obedience to God.

But Jesus clearly taught civilization exit. What happened to complete detachment from systems of power?

Paul taught the opposite. Submit to every authority, integrate, obey. Whether Paul intended this or not, he'd created something emperors could work with.

Then I remembered Constantine. In 313 CE, he legalized Christianity. By 380 CE, it was Rome's official religion.

But why would an emperor adopt a religion founded by a crucified criminal who told people to abandon wealth and serve no master? Unless the version being adopted wasn't from Jesus.

I began researching what Christianity looked like by Constantine's time. The church had already developed hierarchical structures—bishops, councils, centralized authority. And Paul's letters provided the perfect theological framework: Submit to governing authorities ordained by God. Accept social hierarchy as divine will. Obey and receive heavenly reward.

An emperor could work with that. He couldn't work with "sell everything and live like the birds."

This raises the historical question: was Constantine's conversion sincere, or did he simply recognize which religious movement best served his interests?

Either way, the effect was the same. A movement that threatened imperial power became a tool for consolidating it.

Christians were already trained to submit despite incoherence. Already trained to view questioning as spiritual failure. Already trained to obey authorities as if obeying God.

For empire, that's not a bug. That's a feature.

But Christianity wasn't the only religion that succeeded through empire. Islam spread similarly—through rapid military expansion and explicit integration of religious and political authority.

Both religions created empire-compatible frameworks: they taught submission as virtue, made resistance to authority into spiritual rebellion, and turned questioning itself into a threat to salvation. But they added something other major religions lacked: a mandate to convert outsiders, backed by eternal consequences for refusal.

Only Christianity and Islam combine three elements that drive exponential expansion:

1. **Submission framework** (empire-compatible structure)
2. **Conversion mandate** (active expansion requirement)
3. **Eternal punishment for non-believers** (makes concerned believers into relentless conversion agents)

So why did Christianity achieve greater colonial expansion than Islam over the past 400 years?

The evidence suggests it was because Islam was more honest about its demands. The submission aspect was explicit from the start—the name literally means "submission." Though Islam leads with attractive elements like community and spiritual certainty, this upfront transparency created resistance in potential converts.

The other key element appears to be the structural bait-and-switch within Christianity. Missionaries arrived teaching love, grace, and salvation—emphasizing "God so loved the world." They brought medicine, education, and "civilization." The threats came later, after conversion, after psychological investment. Once you'd built your identity around being saved, *then* you learned about eternal torture for leaving, thought crimes, and absolute submission.

The colonial sequence was remarkably consistent: missionaries teach love and service → converts learn indigenous practices are "evil" → European ways become "godly" → resistance becomes spiritual rebellion → political submission follows → empire gains cooperative subjects who believe obedience is virtue.

Not every missionary consciously served imperial interests. In fact, many genuinely opposed exploitation. But the structural result remained the same. The Doctrine of Discovery—papal decrees explicitly authorizing Christian nations to claim non-Christian lands—showed the Church itself had blessed imperial conquest as divine right.

When Jesus taught "take up your cross," his followers understood it as preparation for Rome's terrorizing execution method. But Paul transformed it: "I am crucified with Christ." The cross stopped being a warning about imperial violence and became a badge of spiritual submission. The symbol of Rome's brutality became Christianity's central icon—not as resistance, but as obedience.

I pulled out my Bible and read Jesus's words: "By their fruits you will know them."

What were Christianity's fruits in terms of global power? Centuries of Christian empires, colonial conquest blessed by papal decree, indigenous peoples converted or conquered, cultures and languages lost, hierarchies enforced, and resources extracted. That very same playbook is in action in the jungles of South America at this very moment.

All in the name of a man who told people to abandon wealth and serve no master. I remembered Paul's warning: "Let him become a fool to become wise."

What if we'd been trained to be fools in exactly the way that serves power? What if the "wisdom" we'd learned to reject was simply the capacity to notice when we're being manipulated?

I sat in the pre-dawn darkness, watching the sun rise over the same world Christian empires had shaped for centuries.

By their fruits, indeed.

Chapter 30

Christianity's Legacy

Having traced the imperialistic nature of Christianity, I felt I needed to address the full picture. Despite everything documented in previous chapters, Christianity has positively transformed lives and societies in many ways that rarely get acknowledged these days.

The world can read these words because Protestant reformers challenged Catholic institutional control by promoting vernacular Bible translation and universal literacy. They insisted ordinary people should read scripture themselves rather than depend on church authorities to interpret it for them. The universal education systems that grew from this movement benefit us all today, regardless of religious belief.

Just imagine what your life and our world would be like without common literacy. The Christian literacy movement is especially impactful for me, as I was functionally illiterate until age 16. I believe learning to read may be the single most positively impactful skill for a fruitful life.

The scientific revolution also emerged from Christian theological frameworks. The belief in a rational Creator who designed an ordered universe made systematic investigation meaningful. If God worked through consistent natural laws, those laws could be discovered and understood.

Medieval universities, originally Christian institutions for training clergy, created infrastructure for systematic knowledge preservation. Monasteries preserved classical texts through centuries that might otherwise have lost them entirely.

Many foundational scientists viewed their work as revealing God's design. Newton, Kepler, Galileo, and Boyle saw no contradiction between faith and investigation.

The irony: The same rational inquiry that emerged from Christian theology would later question biblical literalism, miracle claims, the age of the earth, and even Creationism itself.

Though Science undermined many Christian claims, without Christianity, we may not have discovered the scientific method. Just imagine your life without all the benefits that Science has bestowed upon us.

Christians led the fight against the slave trade and played crucial roles in ending slavery in the Americas. Christianity stands out uniquely in organizing systematic, religiously-motivated abolitionist movements. While other religions opposed slavery in various contexts, the scale and sustained nature of Christian anti-slavery activism is unique.

Think about how much suffering was ameliorated because of the abolitionist movement! The courage and love those Christians lived by fills my heart with inspiration and hope for humanity.

Christian hospitals have provided care for the poor and vulnerable for centuries. Christian schools have educated countless people who might otherwise have been denied learning. Christian charitable organizations continue to serve those in need worldwide. Christian leaders like Martin Luther King Jr. drew on their faith to advance civil rights and human dignity. I believe the world is genuinely better because of these actions.

Many of these humanitarian achievements might not have happened without Christianity's influence. The moral courage to challenge entrenched systems of oppression often came from people who took Jesus's teachings about universal love and human dignity seriously.

But Christianity's contributions haven't all been positive. The same scripture that inspired abolitionists also armed devastating religious conflicts. As literacy spread, so did competing certainties about God's will—and the violence to enforce them.

The access to scripture that enabled independent thinking also triggered religious wars that devastated cities and killed millions of Europeans. People read the same texts but reached incompatible conclusions about what they meant.

When texts contain fundamental contradictions, giving more people access to those texts doesn't resolve the contradictions—it just allows more people to choose which version they'll follow and fight over.

The Thirty Years' War devastated Central Europe precisely because both sides could cite scripture to support their positions. Each side believed they were following the true meaning of God's word while their opponents were heretics. The violence came from the certainty that scripture provided clear truth, combined with the reality that it didn't.

The Protestant contribution to literacy was genuine and valuable. But the immediate aftermath showed what happens when millions of people gain access to contradictory authoritative texts—they fragment into competing factions, each certain they've understood correctly.

Fortunately, that era of mass religious warfare is some 400 years in the past, so most modern Christians do not encounter violence from other Christians, but we have all gained from the benefits of Christian causes. What is it that inspired Christianity to take up those transformational causes?

I believe the answer reveals itself when we examine which teachings inspired which outcomes. The humanitarian achievements—abolitionism, hospitals, charitable service, civil rights—flowed from Jesus's teachings about universal love: "love your enemies," "blessed are the merciful," "do to others as you would have them do to you." These emphasize compassion and human dignity without demanding adherence to specific doctrines.

I suspect the violence and persecution came from Jesus's exclusivist claims: demands for absolute belief in him, threats of eternal punishment for incorrect theology, positioning himself as the only path to salvation. When people believed God demanded correct doctrine under threat of damnation, they must have felt justified—even obligated—to enforce orthodoxy through violence.

Both streams of teaching exist in scripture. Both have profoundly shaped history. The question becomes: which teachings will we emphasize?

Chapter 31

Locking the Gate

While researching how the Gutenberg Press spread literacy and made Bibles available in common languages, I found evidence of a possible biblical coverup.

The Catholic Church violently opposed letting ordinary people read the Bible. For over a thousand years, the Church kept scripture in Latin. Only educated clergy could access it. And translating the Bible into languages regular people could understand? That was a death sentence.

John Wycliffe produced the first complete English Bible in the 1380s and died of natural causes in 1384. The Church, however, was not finished with him. In 1415, he was posthumously condemned as a heretic. Forty-four years after his death, in 1428, church officials carried out the sentence: they dug up his corpse, burned his bones, and cast the ashes into the River Swift.

William Tyndale translated the New Testament into English in 1526. He was strangled and burned at the stake in 1536. His last words were reportedly: "Lord, open the King of England's eyes."

In an unexpected twist of history, it appears his prayer was answered. Just two years later, King Henry VIII authorized the Great Bible for use in the Church of England—a translation that was largely Tyndale's own forbidden work.

The Church's stated reason for his execution: preventing "misinterpretation" by uneducated people who might not grasp complex theological truths.

But think about what happened the moment common people gained Bible access during the Protestant Reformation. Christianity immediately fractured into thousands of denominations. Over 40,000 exist today, each reading the same text and reaching different conclusions. It was akin to the sword of division Jesus said he came to bring.

The Catholic Church responded with the Council of Trent (1545-1563), which declared only the Church could interpret scripture correctly. Individual interpretation was condemned. Some guided readings in common languages were permitted, but always under direct priestly supervision.

And right when the Reformation threatened Church authority, apologetics evolved from basic defense into a comprehensive system. Every contradiction received sophisticated explanation. What looked like hypocrisy became "divine mystery." What appeared to be cruelty became "righteous judgment." Narcissistic demands for worship became "appropriate honoring of God's holiness."

The Council of Trent established seminaries in 1563, where clergy trained to answer objections—what I've been calling the "Pastor 2-Step." By the time Bibles reached lay people's hands, an entire defensive infrastructure existed to explain away straightforward readings.

Think about that progression:

First, keep the text away from people. Then, when you can't keep it away anymore, teach people how not to read it straightforwardly.

Make questioning dangerous: "Doubting is from Satan." "Lean not on your own understanding." "The wisdom of this world is foolishness to God."

Create interpretive dependency: Only trained theologians can teach correctly. Individual reading without proper guidance leads to heresy—and death.

The text remained inaccessible, then incomprehensible without institutional interpretation, then dangerous to question.

And all of this happened around texts that, when read straightforwardly using Jesus's own stated standards, reveal the patterns documented in previous chapters.

As psyops expert Chase Hughes puts it, "The hallmark of psychological warfare is when disagreement's off-limits." I've boiled it down to this: *Psychological warfare is that which cannot be questioned.*

What do you think?

If the Bible truly was the benevolent "God-spell"—bringing "Good News" rather than casting a binding spell—wouldn't the Catholic Church have wanted everyone reading it?

Part V

Finding the Bones

Our investigation is nearly complete. Together, we have mapped the contradictory character of Jesus. We have unearthed the radical teachings that felt like they could be the "bones" of truth. And we have followed the trail of evidence through history to see how those teachings were systematically inverted into a religion of empire.

We have turned over every rock and looked in every cranny. And now, we are left standing before the final, most difficult question of all.

Was the entire project a well-intentioned failure? Was a beautiful, liberating teaching simply corrupted by a man named Paul and the forces of history? Or was the contradiction we've witnessed from the very beginning not a sign of corruption, but a sign of a single, coherent, and far more terrifying strategy?

My own hope, the hope that drove me through this entire soul-wrenching process, was for the former. I still wanted to salvage a hero, to find the pure teachings and separate them from the man.

But our discipline as detectives demands that we follow the evidence to its logical conclusion, not just to the one we desire.

In Part V, "Finding the Bones," we will confront the final twist. We will see how the entire narrative, from the Garden of Eden to the cross, from the Sermon on the Mount to the epistles of Paul, snaps into place with a chilling clarity. This is the final act of our detective story.

It is here that we will finally, truly, find the bones. But they may not be what we ever expected.

Chapter 32

The Man Behind the Curtain

After documenting the Church's obfuscations and manipulations in the last chapter, I was reminded of a chapter I'd written but removed from this book early on.

I'd set it aside because I couldn't quite articulate what it meant. It was about the forty years the Israelites spent wandering the desert and their growing desire for a human king.

But first, I need to be honest about my own journey through this investigation.

When I started this book, I believed in divine truth. I *still* believe in divine truth—I experience it directly and regularly.

"I" disappear into undifferentiated awareness, the source of all-that-is, pure consciousness that simply loves without judgment or division. I have no doubt about that reality.

But I no longer believe the Source of beingness has anything to do with the God described in the Bible.

When I began, I assumed the biblical God—however corrupted by institutional interpretation—was pointing toward that same reality I experience. I believed that beneath the contradictions and human distortions found in the Bible, there was authentic divine wisdom.

After documenting the contradictions, the hypocrisies, the narcissistic demands for worship, the deliberate manipulation, the staging of events for glory—I can't see any connection to what I experience as divine truth.

The Man Behind the Curtain

The source of all-that-is doesn't judge, doesn't demand worship, doesn't threaten eternal torture, doesn't change its mind, doesn't need validation. It just IS—pure, undivided, loving presence.

The biblical God judges, demands worship, threatens eternal torture, changes its mind, needs validation throughout the biblical texts—repeatedly.

They're not the same being. They can't be.

And the story of Israel demanding a king crystallized this realization for me. It showed me the exact moment when the fabrication became undeniable.

I'll share what I see. Disagreement is welcome.

The Israelites had been living under what's called the period of Judges—tribal leaders who rose up when needed, usually in times of crisis or war. There was no permanent monarch, no standing army, no central government. According to the biblical narrative, God himself was their king, speaking through prophets and judges.

But the people looked around at neighboring nations. The Philistines had kings. The Moabites had kings. These kingdoms had visible leaders, standing armies, organized military power. When enemies threatened, warrior kings rode at the head of their troops.

What did Israel have? An invisible deity who spoke through priests and prophets. When threats came, they had to wait for God to raise up a judge, who might or might not be a military leader. Can you imagine how vulnerable and possibly embarrassed they felt?

So they came to the prophet Samuel with a demand: "Give us a king to judge us like all the nations have" (1 Sam 8:5).

Samuel was disturbed, so he prayed about it, and God responded through him with a devastating warning:

"He will take your sons and make them serve with his chariots and horses... He will take your daughters to be perfumers and cooks and bakers... He will take the best of your fields and vineyards... You will become his slaves. When that day comes, you will cry out for relief from the king you have chosen, but the Lord will not answer you in that day" (1 Samuel 8:11-18).

God laid it out explicitly: A king will exploit you. Take your children. Confiscate your property. Turn you into servants. And when you regret it, I won't rescue you.

And God said something revealing to Samuel: "It is not you they have rejected, but they have rejected me as their king" (1 Sam 8:7).

The demand for a visible, human king was a rejection of God's direct rule. They wanted what they could see, what they could touch, what looked like power—not a disembodied spirit.

God explicitly rejected human monarchy. He warned them it would enslave them. He took their demand as personal rejection.

Then ... he changed his mind.

He not only allowed them to have a king—he *anointed* one. He blessed Saul through Samuel. He established the Davidic line. And from that line would supposedly come the Messiah—the anointed king who would restore Israel's glory.

Wait. God changes his mind?

An omniscient, unchanging deity issues a clear prohibition, explains in detail why it's harmful, calls it personal rejection—then does it anyway when people keep complaining?

That's negotiation. Compromise. Human adaptation to political pressure.

I just couldn't believe that was God—not the "Infinite" God of the Bible, nor the all-that-is I experience. Infinite beings, timeless beings, do not change.

This was the moment I finally stopped believing the biblical God bore any resemblance to the Allness I experience.

I realized I had been working on a profound misunderstanding all my life. Because of the repeated dreams of Jesus and the Allness experiences, I had equated the two without question.

This was the moment I finally stopped believing any of it was real. Once I realized that, my entire perspective on the story changed.

So let's ask ourselves: what if the whole thing was fabricated?

174

Think about it from the priests' perspective. They had authority because they claimed to speak for an invisible God. The people couldn't see YHWH, couldn't hear him directly—they had to trust the priests to relay his words.

That gave the priests enormous power. But it also made them vulnerable.

When the people looked at surrounding nations with visible warrior kings leading armies, inspiring loyalty, providing tangible leadership—of course they wanted that too. An invisible deity couldn't ride at the head of an army. A disembodied voice couldn't inspire troops in battle.

The people were threatening to reject the entire system.

So the priests faced a crisis. If they said "No, God forbids it" and held firm, the people might reject their authority entirely—might turn to other gods, other systems, other leaders. They needed to adapt.

So they "consulted God"—which means they decided among themselves what to do—and conveniently, "God changed his mind."

They selected Saul, someone whom they could work with, and presented him as God's chosen.

They maintained their authority by positioning themselves as the intermediaries who anointed kings. They avoided a fall from power. The saving grace? They could make *and* break kings by claiming divine authorization.

The king would have military and political power, but the priests would have spiritual authority—the power to declare whether a king had God's blessing or had lost it. It's the age-old story of the King's council that leads through political influence and pulling strings.

The priestly class creates an invisible deity who speaks only through them. When that arrangement becomes inconvenient, the "divine will" mysteriously adapts to circumstances. The priests maintain control by positioning themselves as essential mediators between God and king, between heaven and earth.

This pattern of theological utility likely goes back even further.

What if Moses invented or borrowed the concept of YHWH from ideas he learned in Egypt? The people were desperate and disunified in the desert. Maybe he used YHWH to unify disparate tribes fleeing Egypt. Desperate times—desperate measures. The specific origin doesn't matter as much as recognizing the pattern: A claim of exclusive access to divine authority, used to control populations, adapted when necessary to maintain that control, gradually calcified into genuine belief over generations.

Now play it out in your mind: what begins as conscious fabrication to save the people, once scribed, becomes sincere belief when future generations of scribes read scripture. What if the descendants of the original deceivers believed the story?

The pattern then sustains itself.

The entire biblical system feels like the Wizard of Oz—a man behind a curtain, projecting power, demanding worship, controlling through fear and spectacle, desperately maintaining an illusion that has nothing to do with actual divine reality. But it's not a man. It's not a God. It's a book!

And this brings us back to Jesus.

Whether YHWH was Lucifer impersonating the divine, or simply priests impersonating divine authority, the result is identical:

From a system built on claiming to speak for God while serving ego, power, and control, the story of Jesus "corrects" the problem by digging in further. Now, God is no longer disembodied, but a physical king.

And because we have The Book, which can never be changed, we're stuck with this narcissistic God and his Son. Think about it, billions of people organize their lives around texts produced by this system, following leaders who claim divine authority, supporting policies they believe fulfill prophecy.

What may have begun as a human invention to save the people became a convoluted behemoth, because it was written and preserved.

Whether Jesus is Lucifer's Messiah, whether YHWH is the first ego, or if it is all simple human manipulation for power—the pattern remains the same.

That's what I see. If you disagree, maybe you can at least understand my perspective.

Chapter 33

Breaking the Spell

Why has this pattern remained hidden for so long? We could blame the wall of apologetics built to hide it, but even brilliant minds outside the faith often miss these contradictions. This suggests the issue runs deeper than mere indoctrination. It points to a fundamental mechanism in how the human mind processes—or ignores—uncomfortable truths.

This pattern doesn't start with the New Testament. I thought back to the Genesis story. The moment humans ate from the tree of judgment, what did they fall into? Separation, blame, shame, and manipulation.

Life is confusing, and we're not born with a user manual. We become insecure, and we want to be led or we want to oppose, but doesn't truth get lost in that battle?

We want to follow something, a religion, an ideology, a hero—someone or something, just like the Jews in the desert who wanted a king. Theist, atheist, or agnostic, maybe we are all susceptible to this tendency.

Maybe we do this because much like the ancient Hebrews demanding a king, we don't want to think for ourselves. We don't want to take responsibility for figuring out what life is all about, for directing our own lives, for finding inner peace through integrity.

The real irony is that the biblical narrative presents Jesus as being equivalent to the bronze serpent lifted up as the very thing that's poisoning humanity—following, judging, and dividing ourselves. Instead of recognizing the demonstration, so many of us worshipped the demonstrator, it seems.

Could this avoidance of responsibility explain our current global dysfunction? The environmental destruction, endless wars, economic exploitation, political corruption—what if it all stems from insecurity and lack of spiritual maturation?

I believe we are seeing the same pattern Adam and Eve fell into—the same pattern every empire has repeated. The same pattern the majority of the Gospels and Paul's epistles reflect.

Maybe this pattern will continue until we recognize it. Maybe we need to see what has been poisoning us to be healed.

As a world society, it seems to me that we're still eating from the tree of judgment. Maybe that's why we didn't notice this pattern in the Gospels. We've been eating the forbidden fruit, the knowledge of good and evil for too long.

For thousands of years, haven't we been trying to solve the same puzzle? How do we judge who is good and who is evil more accurately?

What if the issue isn't that we judge incorrectly, but that we judge others at all? What if eating from the tree of judgment wasn't about moral failing, but about humans becoming condemnatory?

It seems the insecure mind *likes* judging. It feels somehow good in the moment. It offers a twisted sense of power and control. Do you know what I mean?

But it's false, and maybe destructive—to our souls, to our families, and to our societies.

According to Genesis, every mind that divides reality into good and evil, right and wrong, worthy and unworthy, is eating from the forbidden tree. I have seen it in my own life. Haven't you?

Then a thought arose that both disturbed and inspired me: if we could all be this blind to something so obvious, what else might we be missing? What other Clark Kent glasses are hiding truths from us?

Regarding Jesus, I suppose it would be easy to believe his entire story was made up, or maybe that he was just an insane cult leader. But our belief does not make it so.

That said, even if Jesus never existed, and even if none of its members realize it, Christianity still involves the same practices we discussed earlier.

Even if the entire story is fiction, early Christians somehow designed those rituals, those symbols, those psychological techniques. They created this comprehensive system that has billions of believing members around the world.

Think of how many people might be performing those rituals every week. Seeking to be possessed by the Holy Ghost, ritually consuming symbolic flesh and blood, kneeling in submission, and wearing execution symbols. Where did those practices originate?

Still, I found myself wondering: does this analysis miss something crucial? Christians see something beautiful in these rituals, something sacred. What if their genuine reverence transforms what the practices are for them?

And then a more troubling question: don't Satan worshippers also believe their practices are sacred? Don't they feel blessed and connected to the divine? I don't know, but I bet they do.

Maybe *sacred* means vastly different things to different people. Is the sacred feeling of a Satanist the same as the sacred feeling of a Christian? I doubt it.

Then a disturbing thought arose. Sacred feelings can be manufactured. If the sense of divine presence can be simulated, then it could be used for deception.

That would mean every religion, every spiritual practice, every person who feels blessed or guided could potentially be experiencing a sophisticated counterfeit.

And if that's true, then spiritual experience alone isn't a reliable guide. Something else is needed.

How do we know our sense of alignment with God isn't just another sophisticated deception?

And as soon as I asked the question, something occurred to me. Maybe we only need to ask ourselves what the experience actually produces in our lives.

Does it lead toward integrity, or does it split me? Make me say one thing and do another?

Does it create unity or separation in my relationships? Us versus them thinking?

Does it free me from judgment, or does it potentiate judgment and condemnation?

Does it inspire sincerity, or performance? Defending and justifying?

Does it lead to independence, or lead to dependency on leaders and saviors?

Does it welcome questions, or make me avoid anything that might challenge the belief?

Maybe that's the test. Not how the sacred feels, but what it actually produces.

Wholeness or fragmentation? Unity or separation? Independence or dependency? Maybe the fruit really does tell the truth.

What strikes me as truly freeing about this line of reasoning: we don't need an intermediary to discern spiritual truth. We don't need a priest or pastor or guru.

We have everything we need right inside us, the capacity to see whether something leads to wholeness or division, freedom or bondage. Maybe that's our direct connection to Truth.

And perhaps many sincere Christians are already using this inner discernment—their conscience leads them past problematic elements toward something universal: love, service, integrity, forgiveness. Maybe practitioner intention really is the most pivotal thing.

What gives me hope is that I've met Christians whose lives seem to embody genuine love, service, and compassion. They focus on helping others, caring for the vulnerable, and building community—inspired by the Sermon on the Mount.

What if these sincere believers, by following their moral compass rather than every biblical detail, have been leading a more spiritual life than they could if they followed the Bible more strictly? What if their instinct to emphasize love over judgment, service over power, and mercy over manipulation represents a genuine path to wholeness?

Maybe the Christians who've "overlooked" the darker passages and focused on love have been living a spiritually fulfilling path all along.

I suppose my largest concern is this: In seeing the contradictions and potential deceptions within Christianity, some people may entirely reject all spiritual growth frameworks.

Our societies already show concerning signs of spiritual abandonment. Extended adolescence, widespread nihilism, and doubt about humanity's value suggest many have lost connection to transcendent meaning. When people view humanity as inherently destructive—a "cancer on the earth"—extinction can seem preferable to the demanding work of individual and collective growth.

Many of Jesus's teachings demand more responsibility, not less. Love, non-judgment, and integrity require extraordinary discipline—the opposite of self-absorption.

Whether through religious frameworks or secular paths, humans may need structures that challenge them to take responsibility for their lives, relationships, and contributions to civilization.

Maybe Jesus's dream of immortality is unrealistic, but love, non-judgment, and integrity—they seem like a perfect recipe for spiritual growth.

The demographic crisis around the world, where people do not have enough children to sustain their populations, reflects, in part, a loss of meaning that makes the sacrifices of raising families seem pointless. My prayer is that this investigation does not contribute to that spiritual void.

The human spirit calls us toward something greater than immediate gratification. But we must distinguish between frameworks that genuinely serve human flourishing versus those that create dependency through manipulation.

It seems to me true spirituality directs us to take complete responsibility for becoming the humans we're capable of being.

What happens to humanity if we fail to live up to that directive?

Chapter 34

The Bones of Life

As I sat in my office, staring at the contradictions and manipulations documented in hundreds of pages, the evidence of an Ego-based system masquerading as divine truth, I remembered that I had started this investigation with a promise.

Find my bones. They are the core of my teaching. Most of what is written about me is untrue. Mankind has twisted my message for selfish gain, until almost nothing of its essence remains.

Had I found that essence, those bones? As I reached the end of my biblical exploration, I uncovered something: buried beneath all the contradictions, manipulations, and institutional capture, there were teachings that felt different— clean, whole, undivided.

I reflected on the immortality teachings. You'd have to stake your entire life on being immortal even to test those teachings. Half-measures, it seems, would never get you there.

Maybe that's why I have never met a single Christian who sold everything they had and lived like the birds, dedicating their entire lives to worship the Lord. Have you? That's largely due to Paul's influence, I suspect.

Could one truly live like the birds, storing nothing, preparing for nothing, having no possessions whatsoever, giving away everything to whomever asked? Can one truly move a mountain with one's word? Does living a totally celibate life lead to immortality?

I'm not sure Jesus proved it. Nor am I sure he proved he was God or even the Messiah. But that doesn't mean there is nothing of value in his teachings, does it?

Sitting with all I'd discovered, I found myself looking for something that felt clean and whole, something that leads us beyond Ego.

And there it was scattered throughout the Sermon on the Mount. Those passages that had sustained me since childhood:

"Love your enemies, bless those who curse you, do good to those who hate you, and pray for those who mistreat you and persecute you."

"Therefore, whatever you desire for men to do to you, you shall also do to them; for this is the law and the prophets."

"Don't judge, and you won't be judged. Don't condemn, and you won't be condemned. Set free, and you will be set free."

These teachings don't seek glory. They don't demand worship. They don't create psychological traps. They simply point toward a way of being.

I wrote them out, one after another:

- o Judge not; condemn not; set free
- o Love universally, including enemies
- o Forgive absolutely
- o Do unto others as you'd have them do to you
- o Let your yes be yes and your no be no (align word and action)
- o The truth will set you free (alignment with reality rather than comfortable delusion)

These weren't separate teachings. They were all expressions of one fundamental shift: **Stop dividing reality through judgment and falsehood.**

What if this fruit was of the tree of life?

I thought back to Genesis as a metaphoric allegory. We could look at the fall itself as eating from the tree of the knowledge of good and evil—the capacity to judge, to fragment reality into worthy and unworthy, right and wrong, us and them.

YHWH demonstrated judgment consciousness: creating hierarchies, demanding worship, punishing rivals. Lucifer mirrored the same pattern: seeking glory, requiring submission, judging and condemning.

Both were trapped in the same fragmented consciousness. But "judge not" pointed to something different entirely. When you cease judgment, everything else follows naturally:

- o **Love becomes universal** because no one is judged unworthy of love.
- o **Forgiveness becomes automatic** because no one needs to be punished for failing your standards.
- o **The golden rule emerges naturally** because you're not maintaining separate standards for yourself and others.
- o **Integrity becomes effortless** because you're not performing for approval or defending against condemnation.

Rather than being moral achievements, these practices return us to undivided being. I sat back, in awe of the simplicity.

The entire investigation had been about judgment—tracing how YHWH judged, how Lucifer judged, how Jesus judged or didn't judge, how Paul taught judgment, how Christianity enforced judgment through threat of damnation.

And the solution had been there all along, in the simplest teaching: **Judge not.** Not "judge correctly" or "judge fairly"—just stop fragmenting reality.

I thought about my own experience of what I call the source of being. That undifferentiated awareness that exists before and beneath all stories, all identities, all divisions. It doesn't judge. It simply is.

Maybe that's what Jesus was pointing toward. Not a theological system. Not a set of rules. Just a return to undivided consciousness.

These teachings work regardless of whether Jesus was historical, whether he was the Cosmic Ego, whether miracles are true, or whether the Bible is accurate.

They work because they address the fundamental fracture in human consciousness—the judgment that divides us from ourselves, each other, and the source of being.

Maybe these are the bones. The core teaching that survived all the corruption, all the theological manipulation, all the institutional capture.

Stop judging. Love. Forgive. Live with integrity.

Everything else—all the complexity, all the theology, all the institutional religion—could be set aside, and we'd be better for it.

I thought about how different the world might be if Christianity had emphasized these teachings rather than the dependency teachings that demand worship under threat of torture.

What if churches taught: "Judge not" as the fundamental practice?

What if instead of converting people through fear of hell, they simply demonstrated radical love and integrity?

What if the message was: "Stop dividing reality. Return to wholeness. That's salvation"?

But that wouldn't create empires, would it?

You can't build hierarchies on "judge not." You can't demand submission based on universal love. You can't create us-versus-them when everyone is equally worthy of compassion.

They're profoundly threatening to any system based on judgment and hierarchy. Including, apparently, most of what became Christianity.

I looked at the notes from my childhood dreams one more time.

Find my bones.

Here they are, I thought—simple, radical, undivided.

Judge not. Love all. Forgive completely. Live with integrity.

These teachings don't require belief in any supernatural claims. They don't demand theological agreement. They simply invite us to stop dividing ourselves through judgment.

And maybe—just maybe—that return to wholeness is what humans have been needing all along. Not salvation through belief or escape through worship, but the end of judgment and the return to undivided being.

The bones of life itself.

Chapter 35

A Child's Wisdom

As I sat in contemplation, I wondered what Jesus really stood for and whether he resurrected. Of course, I highly doubt it. Let's consider what would happen if Jesus did not resurrect.

Maybe the inconsistent resurrection accounts in the four Gospels aren't evidence of supernatural events, but independent attempts to save a movement built on a failed promise. That would explain their incredible inconsistencies.

A lot of Christians died for their faith, due to persecution. So maybe once people began dying for these fabricated stories, admitting that maybe Jesus did not resurrect became next to impossible.

Psychologists call this inability the sunk cost fallacy—the tendency to continue investing in something that isn't working because you've already invested so much that walking away feels like admitting total failure.

The more you've sacrificed for a belief, the harder it becomes to abandon it, even when evidence shows it's false, and especially if it has led to the suffering and death of many.

Imagine early Christians: they'd left their families, given up their livelihoods, endured persecution, all because they believed Jesus would demonstrate immortality through resurrection. When he died and stayed dead, admitting failure meant their entire lives had been based on a lie.

Imagine if you convinced your family and friends to join, and some of them died because of their belief. Can you imagine admitting the truth that you misled someone into dying for a false belief?

Guilt can turn rationality into the enemy in circumstances like that. Maybe creating resurrection stories was psychologically easier than facing the devastating truth.

When your concept of the divine already includes domination, judgment, and demanding worship, egoic behavior becomes indistinguishable from godliness.

Early Christians, raised on Greek and Roman mythology where gods were jealous, vengeful, and demanding, may not have seen anything strange about a divine Jesus who threatens eternal punishment and demands absolute worship. Maybe they were simply applying their cultural understanding of what gods do.

Maybe Christianity, rather than escaping paganism, incorporated pagan concepts of divinity and called them holy. Zeus demanding worship becomes the Father. Hades becomes Hell. Divine wrath becomes righteous judgment.

As I sat with these thoughts, I realized this investigation had revealed something beyond ancient texts. The patterns we'd uncovered were still playing out everywhere around us.

I remembered the childhood confusion I'd felt when adults rationalized contradictions in revered figures, in their political party, in their heroes. Something had always bothered me about the way we bend rules for those we identify with.

It seems to me that many children detect hypocrisy instinctively. They know when something is unfair.

My theory is this: when children witness adults making excuses for revered figures, a gradual process begins. Most children slowly acclimate to the contradictions. They learn to suppress their natural sense of fairness to fit in, to avoid the discomfort of questioning what everyone else accepts.

This same pattern, or what I've been calling the "pastor two-step," warps how we think about ethics everywhere. If we can excuse judgment in a divine teacher who preached "judge not," we learn to excuse hypocrisy in leaders, in systems, in ourselves.

No wonder human societies struggle so much with accountability. Without universal accountability, politicians, executives, and elites float above the standards we apply to ordinary people. It seems we've been trained from childhood to look away when authority figures break their own rules. "It's different for them," we say, echoing the same rationalizations that shielded biblical inconsistencies.

I found myself wondering: What if we stopped making exceptions? What if integrity really meant no loopholes?

I need to pause here and share something I had entirely forgotten until now.

I can remember the tremendous fear I felt as a child when my Bible study teacher told me that my parents would burn in hell for eternity because they were not born-again Christians.

She told me it was my responsibility to make them believers. Unless they accepted Jesus into their hearts as their Lord and Savior, they would suffer the fires of hell forever.

I can clearly remember my tremendous love for them and a matching terror. Their eternal lives were in my hands.

How could I get them to believe in Jesus? I was just a boy. I had no idea what to do. It was a horrible, crushing feeling—being told that the people I loved most in the world faced eternal torment, and that somehow it was up to me to save them.

Years later, I learned what happened to that Bible study teacher.

Her husband had lost trust in her because she had been secretly trying to get the entire neighborhood's children to convert their parents, despite promising him she wouldn't do that. When the parents complained and he found out, their marriage began to spiral apart.

She had been a stay-at-home mom in a wealthy household, living a very comfortable life. She lost it all.

Years later my best childhood friend told me he saw her in a McDonald's with another man, wearing a post office uniform, smoking cigarettes and frequently cursing. She had completely lost her faith and looked haggard.

The woman who had once terrorized children with visions of hell had herself fallen from grace.

But now I feel tremendous gratitude. In her misguided zeal to save souls, she planted in me something far more valuable than the certainty she preached.

188

A Child's Wisdom

The terror of that childhood moment launched a lifelong search that led not to the faith she demanded, but to faith in the search, faith in questioning, faith in the possibility that truth might be found, not through any specific form of faith, but through faith in truth itself, even if we can't always articulate it.

That memory connected back to those dreams of Jesus, his profound sorrow perhaps reflecting what happens when we worship the very patterns that divide us. Maybe healing starts when we hold everyone—including our most revered figures—to the same unflinching standards.

I imagined what that might look like: No more divided hearts. No more blind worship. Just honest, undivided living.

The implications felt staggering. If we could see through the oldest, most protected deceptions, what else might become possible?

And that brings us to Lucifer: let's imagine he is a real being for a moment.

Maybe the greatest trick the Devil ever pulled wasn't convincing the world he didn't exist but convincing the world that he is God.

In doing so, he's trapped himself. After all, isn't Ego the ultimate spiritual trap?

Think about it: Lucifer is trapped in a constant act. That's what it means to be trapped in Ego, right? It must be so exhausting constantly seeking attention, constantly trying to be seen and worshipped. It's so sad.

As I sat with the thought that even Lucifer might be trapped in the very ego-pattern he represents, I experienced a deep realization. All the months of investigation, all the contradictions I'd traced, all the patterns I'd documented—they weren't just about ancient texts anymore.

I could see the same dynamics playing out in my own mind. And in that moment of seeing my own pattern so clearly, I felt something shift within me.

It's such a strange feeling, really—this feeling that if it's about your identity in any way, it's ego. Maybe that's the deceiver.

And then I had an insight. Elohim, or whatever we call the origin of All-That-Is, has no Ego and is thus not trying to be seen.

Maybe that's why we tend not to notice.

Chapter 36

The Final Twist

I thought the investigation was over. I had traced the patterns, documented the contradictions, and followed the story to what seemed to be its end: a divine narrative that unravels under scrutiny, a possibly hijacked religion, and, buried beneath it all, the precious bones of universal truth. I felt a sense of somber completion.

Then, a conversation with one of my martial arts students shook my perspective.

He is a devout Christian, and I told him of my project. He listened carefully, his expression earnest. "Sensei," he began, "I respect the path you're on, but I think you're missing something. You keep trying to find two Jesuses in the Bible—a good one and a bad one. But there's only one. You have to take all of it, or none of it."

I explained my findings, the conflicting voices, the clear difference between the Sermon on the Mount and the man who cursed a fig tree. He listened patiently, then shook his head. "It's all the same Jesus," he insisted. "You just can't see it yet."

I couldn't see it. To me, the contradictions were the whole story. I thanked him for his perspective, and we left it at that. But his certainty—his simple, unshakeable belief in a unified narrative—stuck with me. It felt like a stone in my shoe.

Weeks passed. As I prepared the final manuscript, his words kept echoing. *There's only one.* My entire investigation had been an effort to separate the clean from the corrupt, the authentic from the inauthentic. It was driven by the hope I'd carried since childhood, the hope that beneath the layers of religion, the true Jesus of my dreams could be found.

And then, a thought surfaced that made my stomach drop.

I had subjected the Bible to an unflinching analysis, giving no special exemptions. But had I, in the end, given one to myself? Had I allowed my own hope—my desire to find the "bones" and preserve a benevolent teaching—to become its own rose-colored lens? In my effort to exonerate a "good Jesus" from the actions of a "bad Jesus" and the inversions of Paul, I had still been trying to save a hero.

I had to ask myself the hardest question of all. What if my student was right? What if there was only one biblical Jesus? And what if the contradictions weren't a sign of corruption, but of a single, coherent, and far more disturbing strategy?

I took a deep breath and forced myself to look at my own conclusions from a new angle. What if the Second Exodus was not a well-intentioned failure? What if its radical purity, its impossible standard, wasn't a mark of its divinity, but of its malevolence? And what if the bones I had identified were the bait?

Suddenly, the entire narrative snapped into place with a chilling clarity. The most effective deception is not a lie, but a truth that conceals a hook. The teachings I had identified as the "bones"—to love universally, to forgive absolutely, to judge not—are indeed the core of every genuine spiritual path on earth. We see them in the words of the Buddha, in the heart of the African teachings of Ubuntu. They are real. They are true.

And that is precisely what made them the perfect bait.

What if the plan was not to invent a new lie, but to take the most profound truth of undivided being and claim exclusive ownership of it? A universal truth was welded to a non-universal, egoic condition: the hook. The message became, "This path to liberation is real, but you can only walk it *through me*." What if the teaching of unity was used to create the ultimate division: the saved versus the damned, those who are "in Christ" and those who are cast out.

Through this new lens, I could see that Jesus and Paul may not have been in conflict at all. Maybe they represent two stages of a single, brilliant plan. Let's imagine the strategy and see where it takes us.

Stage One (Jesus): He introduces the bait. He preaches a radical, impossible purity—the Second Exodus—that was designed to fail. Its very impossibility would create the necessary chaos, attract the most devoted and desperate souls, and set the stage for the creation of the ultimate martyr.

Stage Two (Paul): Paul arrives after the inevitable failure of Stage One. Guided by a vision of Jesus on the road to Damascus, Paul provides the "practical" solution: the institutional framework, the rules for society, the theology that could be integrated with empire. Maybe Paul didn't corrupt the original mission; maybe he *completed* it. He built the vessel designed to carry the martyr myth across the world.

But why? If the goal was simply to be worshiped, why create a system that, as I had seen in my research, seems to be heading for the self-destruction of its own followers? It didn't make sense, until I realized that maybe the goal was never worship. Maybe worship was just the mechanism.

I remembered the oral teachings of Christianity, found in writings like Milton's *Paradise Lost* and C.S. Lewis's modern evangelical sermons. Maybe this was the final piece of the puzzle.

According to these teachings, the Devil's true goal was to prove God wrong about his creation. To show that humanity was unworthy of divine love. Just about any studied Christian could tell you this.

If proving humanity flawed was the Devil's true aim, what better proof could there be than to hand humanity the keys to its own liberation—love, forgiveness, non-judgment—and watch them use those very keys to build a religion of judgment, division, and holy war? To lead them to a final, self-inflicted "Day of Judgment"—Armageddon, all in the name of God?

With this piece of the puzzle in place, the fractured voices had merged into one. Maybe my student was right. There was only one Jesus in the Gospels. A singular, patient, and terrifyingly coherent figure who played the part of the "Savior" so brilliantly, offering the truth of heaven to lead humanity into a hell of its own making.

Maybe the plan was not flawed. Maybe it was perfect. The most beautiful teachings were the most dangerous part of the trap, and the bones I had been searching for my entire life were the bait.

192

If it was a plan, the mind behind it would have to be devious in ways unimaginable. Faced with such a potent design, one has to ask: Is the figure of Lucifer more than just a literary device? Is he real?

But after much consideration, I realized the answer doesn't change the outcome.

It ultimately doesn't matter if Lucifer is a real being plotting our doom from some fiery throne. The men who wrote this book, whether divinely inspired or tragically misguided, created a textual virus that accomplishes the exact same effect.

They captured the pattern of the ultimate Ego in ink, and in doing so, they made it immortal. The Bible itself became the serpent, lifted up for all to see, poisoning humanity with the very idea of a God who judges, divides, and demands worship.

And that brings us to the question of Jesus's true identity. In the end, the character of Jesus, as written, remains a master of plausible deniability. The text is constructed in such a way that he never quite confesses, yet the pattern is undeniable.

He is like a figure seen through a fractured mirror. From one angle, you see the sublime teacher, the healer, the man of compassion. From another, you see the pattern of the Cosmic Ego—the being who demands total submission, seeks glory at the expense of others, and orchestrates events to prove his own divinity.

So, I cannot be the one to close this case file. You have seen the evidence. You have heard the testimony. You have seen the contradictions and the chilling coherence of the "Bait and Trap" theory.

I leave it to you, dear reader, to render the final verdict. Who is this man?

Author's Note: *I want to acknowledge how difficult this final twist might be to consider. For me, it was horrific. I spent this entire investigation holding onto the hope of finding a pure, benevolent teaching to salvage, and the investigation demanded I question even that hope. But in that struggle, I found a strange kind of hope. If you see the "bait," you see the "bones." Strip away the poison, and the core teachings stand free: clean, universal, and life-giving. Seeing the possibility of a trap is not the end of the journey. For me, it felt like the final, necessary step before true freedom becomes possible.*

Chapter 37

A Living Example

After finishing this manuscript, I knew I needed professional help. The implications of this material were too staggering. I had to be sure the logic held up.

I found an editor with a background in biblical scholarship and explained the book's premise. Would his Christian faith prevent him from engaging fairly? He assured me he could work objectively, regardless of personal beliefs.

"I want you to poke holes in this if there are any," I told him. "Subject it to intense scrutiny, but do not use apologetics to do so. If there are flaws in my reasoning, I need to know."

What happened next surprised me.

Despite my explicit statement that we would give Jesus "no special exemptions," the editor immediately began making them. Every contradiction I'd documented was explained away. My observations were dismissed as "idiosyncratic and not borne out by the texts." When I pressed on specific points, he replied, "It's hyperbole." "You don't understand the Jewish context." "The Church always taught this correctly."

When I noted that Jesus said, "judge not" then called people "hypocrites" and "liars," the response was telling: "Jesus is God, and therefore God is allowed to judge!" This was exactly the "God-pass" the entire book was designed to avoid.

But his response was a symptom of a deeply ingrained interpretive system that runs completely counter to the straight-forward approach this book has taken. The traditional biblical reading operates under a set of implicit, unwritten rules— the foundational principles of apologetics. In retrospect, I can articulate them:

1. Start with the Conclusion: The analysis must begin with the axiom that Jesus is divine, perfect, and good. Any evidence to the contrary is flawed, not the conclusion.
2. Harmonize, Don't Contradict: If two passages conflict, the goal is not to document the contradiction but to find a "higher," more complex interpretation that makes them agree.
3. Explain Away, Don't Scrutinize: Apparent moral failings are not evidence of a flawed character but opportunities to understand a "deeper" theological truth (e.g., righteous anger, divine will, a misunderstood metaphor).
4. The "God-Pass" is Always Valid: The ultimate escape hatch for any ethical or logical inconsistency is "His ways are not our ways." God is not bound by the rules He gives to humanity.

My editor, like thousands of theologians and saints before him, was operating under these rules. His intellect wasn't engaging with the evidence presented; it was deploying a pre-packaged defense system designed to protect a conclusion he already held. This is why our conversation was so startling. I was trying to have a discussion about evidence, while he was compelled by his training to perform apologetics. We were operating under two mutually exclusive sets of rules for what it means to read honestly.

This programming became undeniable when I presented the most astonishing fact of all: that the New Testament identifies Jesus with the title of the Morning Star.

The editor's response was automatic. He said, "Jesus is the true morning star, who replaces the devil. Do you actually think that people who have read the Bible are not aware that Jesus called himself the morning star, which is also a title for Lucifer? It's right there in the text . . . everyone who has read the Bible has noticed it. Do you see how this is not a discovery?"

His dismissal was a perfect example of Rule #3 in action: *Explain Away, Don't Scrutinize.* Rather than engage with the textual evidence from Isaiah and Revelation, he asserted a theological conclusion—"Jesus replaces the devil"—as if it were fact, effectively overriding the scripture itself.

His response left me wondering: do people truly realize that the Bible identifies Jesus with the fallen Morning Star? I think if they knew that before becoming Christian, they might choose a different path.

If my editor was correct that this connection was widely known, surely scripture would make it clear. To put my heart at ease, I searched the Bible for any statement indicating Jesus came to redeem the title of the Morning Star.

I found nothing. I then searched the internet and discovered that others, as my editor claimed, had indeed questioned whether Jesus was the Devil. Christian defenders consistently claimed "Jesus replaced Satan," but in every case, they omitted any scriptural evidence for these assertions.

If such a fundamental theological distinction existed in scripture, wouldn't it be prominently cited? Apologetics doesn't allow this question.

Due to how Christians have been conditioned to think about scripture through apologetics, even intelligent, well-intentioned people become unable to examine evidence objectively. Their intellect transforms into a defense system when core beliefs are challenged.

His other responses I found equally revealing: "If Jesus is just a man, then the Gospels are completely pointless and uninteresting." He literally could not conceive of examining Jesus without presupposing divinity.

But his dismissal also revealed something troubling about Christian conditioning. This is the same attitude many Christians display toward the founders of other religions like Lao Tzu or Buddha—"They're just human, but Jesus is God"—as if human wisdom has no value whatsoever.

Think about it: Socrates, Aristotle, Buddha, Lao Tzu—all "just human," yet their insights have guided humanity for millennia. But this editor couldn't conceive of finding value in a human Jesus.

This conditioning isn't unique to my editor. Even C.S. Lewis, one of Christianity's most respected apologists, recognized the logical problem inherent in the Gospel narratives. In *Mere Christianity*, Lewis wrote:

> *I am trying here to prevent anyone saying the really foolish thing that people often say about Him: I'm ready to accept Jesus as a great moral teacher, but I don't accept his claim to be God. That is the one thing we must not say. A man who was merely a man and said the sort of things Jesus said would not be a great moral teacher. He would either be a lunatic—on the level with the man who says he is a poached egg—or else he would be the Devil of Hell.*

A Living Example

Lewis intended this as proof that Jesus must be God, but notice what he's unintentionally admitting: taken at face value, the Gospel Jesus displays characteristics that could indicate "the Devil of Hell" rather than divine harmony.

Lewis's own logic leads to the very conclusion my textual analysis reached, but he could not see it. Such is the power of apologetics. But if we follow Lewis's thinking to its logical conclusion, this isn't just a reflection of Jesus—it's a reflection of **YHWH** himself:

- Like the Cosmic Ego, the LORD is jealous.
- Like the Cosmic Ego, the LORD demands worship.
- Like the Cosmic Ego, the LORD punishes eternally for the finite crime of not believing in him or his chosen Messiah.

The behavioral patterns are identical. And this brings me back to the question my father asked me when I was eight years old—the question that started this whole journey.

When faced with the threat of eternal hell, he didn't try to rationalize it like Lewis. He simply asked: *"Would you love or respect a God that would send people to Hell just for being of a different religion?"*

Even as a child, I knew the answer was "No."

That is the ultimate irony: an eight-year-old's simple moral clarity was more reliable than the sophisticated theology of Christianity's greatest defender. I realized I would not respect that God. In fact, I wouldn't even like that God.

That conversation with my father launched a lifelong search for truth that led, eventually, to the investigation you've just read. It took decades of maturation and analysis to return to the simple moral clarity I possessed as a child—that genuine divinity would never demand worship through terror, never torture finite beings for eternity, and never ask us to justify narcissism and malice simply because the authority figure we are aligned with is performing it.

The dreams of Jesus that began after that conversation showed me a figure of infinite love and compassion—nothing like the judgmental deity of orthodox Christianity. Maybe that's what happens when we stop worshipping the twisted version of divinity that religious authorities have constructed and start listening to the voice that speaks in moral clarity rather than theological complexity.

The Unauthorized Jesus

The question my father asked me still echoes: "Would you love or respect a God that would send people to Hell just for being of a different religion?"

I still wouldn't. Would you?

And then it hit me—the Christian dismissal that Jesus would be "pointless and uninteresting" without being God may have inadvertently revealed how Christianity became the distorted message it seems to be.

Unable to find value in Jesus as a man, they felt compelled to make him divine. But their concept of divinity—demanding worship, threatening eternal torture, requiring blood sacrifice—was already distorted. So when they deified Jesus, they may have unwittingly turned him into the Cosmic Ego.

Given the incredible power of apologetics, I doubt devout Christians can see the egoic aspects of Christianity, even when it is pointed out to them. They may think that's what God looks like.

Imagine an intelligent, curious youth reading the New Testament. They are likely to read it as a true story. If this youth holds Jesus to his own stated standards, imagining that miracles happen, God and Lucifer are real, heaven and hell are actual spiritual dimensions, and that there is an ongoing spiritual war for our souls, they will probably notice the rampant hypocrisy, even if they love Jesus for his miracles.

But the harsh reality for children is that questioning the narrative is considered unacceptable. Consider what this does to our youth. We learn not to trust our inner compass. We learn to defer to authority, even when it makes no sense. We learn to follow the crowd for acceptance.

As my editor stressed: "You can't read it that way."

Why not?

May truth set us free,

Richard L Haight

Postscript

The Summoning

Our investigation into the texts is complete. We have found the bones. But if we stop here, this entire book will have been a mere intellectual exercise. We must now take the pattern we have identified—the Cosmic Ego that demands worship and divides humanity—and overlay it onto our current reality to see the fruit of the story.

This brings us to the ongoing wars and tensions in the Middle East. After documenting the power of blind belief, I knew the issue ran much deeper than resources and land, and I suspected the issue wasn't solely the religious fervor of "Islamic extremists."

The term "Zionism" arose repeatedly in the news. I knew very little about it, so I researched it. It's the thread that unravels the façade.

Did you know there are three completely different versions of Zionism? Understanding the distinction is the key to understanding why American foreign policy in the Middle East often seems to contradict American interests. It might also be the key to understanding why we're closer to nuclear war than at any point in human history.

The first version is **Political Zionism**, which is the belief that Jewish people should have a homeland in their ancestral territory. This movement emerged in the late 1800s, largely in response to violent persecution of Jews throughout Europe and Russia.

After the Holocaust demonstrated the catastrophic consequences of statelessness, Political Zionism gained international support. The United

Nations voted to partition Palestine, based on the Balfour Declaration of 1917. In 1948, the modern state of Israel was established.

Political Zionism is fundamentally about Jewish self-determination and safety. You can agree or disagree with specific policies of the Israeli government while recognizing why many Jews see Israel as essential to their survival.

This isn't the Zionism I'm exploring in this chapter.

The second version is **Religious Zionism**, also called the National Religious movement. While Political Zionism emerged as a modern response to persecution, Religious Zionism operates from biblical theology that's thousands of years old.

Religious Zionists—primarily Orthodox and ultra-Orthodox Jews—believe that establishing and expanding Israel is a divine commandment. For them, the return to Israel and the settlement of biblical territories fulfills God's covenant with Abraham and hastens the coming of the Messiah.

The biblical foundation comes from Genesis 15:18-21, where God promises Abraham's descendants land "from the river of Egypt to the great river, the river Euphrates." This encompasses not just current Israel and Palestine, but Lebanon, Syria, parts of Jordan, Iraq, and parts of Egypt.

This vision of maximal territorial expansion is often referred to as "Greater Israel," a concept embraced by the most extreme religious Zionists as a literal divine mandate that justifies settlement growth and resists any compromise on biblical lands. It requires the removal of all non-Jews, including Arabs and Christians, to create a pure ethno-state.

The question is, does Israeli leadership identify with this vision?

During a live interview on Israel's i24 News channel on August 12, 2025, host Sharon Gal presented Prime Minister Benjamin Netanyahu with a custom gold pendant engraved with a map outlining "Greater Israel." Netanyahu accepted the gift, holding it up to the camera, and said it was intended for his wife, Sara. He described it as "the map of the Promised Land" and, when Gal asked if he "connects to the vision," replied, "Very much so."

I was surprised to learn that significant elements of Israeli leadership—particularly in Prime Minister Benjamin Netanyahu's far-right coalition—openly identify with the "Greater Israel" vision, viewing it as a blend of biblical mandate, historical right, and security imperative.

That interview has been clipped, memed, and weaponized across social media, turning "From the river to the sea, Palestine will be free" into a louder rallying cry amid the backlash.

While most Political Zionists don't advocate for these maximal borders, Religious Zionists view the biblical promise as a literal divine grant that cannot be negotiated away. To them, every settlement built, every inch of land claimed, every step toward rebuilding the Temple represents obedience to God.

This isn't a fringe belief. Religious Zionists represent a significant portion of Israeli society and wield substantial political influence. Movements like Gush Emunim (Block of the Faithful) have driven settlement expansion throughout the West Bank. Organizations like the Temple Institute have spent decades preparing for the Third Temple's construction.

For Religious Zionists, compromise on territorial claims is betraying God's covenant. Peace negotiations that would require giving up land are seen as spiritually intolerable, regardless of political or humanitarian consequences.

This theological framework makes rational negotiation nearly impossible. How do you compromise on what you believe God explicitly commanded? How do you trade land for peace when you believe the land itself is a divine gift that hastens the coming of the Messiah?

The difference between Political and Religious Zionism is critical: Political Zionists might accept territorial compromise for security. Religious Zionists cannot, because their framework defines such compromise as sin against God.

The third version is **Christian Zionism**, and it operates from an entirely different motivation.

Christian Zionists support Israel not primarily out of concern for Jewish safety or self-determination, but because they believe establishing and maintaining the state of Israel is a necessary step in triggering biblical prophecy, specifically, the return of Jesus Christ and the Day of Judgment.

When I first learned about this, I assumed it was fringe theology. Then I looked at the numbers.

Approximately 25-30% of Americans identify as Evangelical Christians. Within that group, surveys suggest a significant majority, upwards of 60-80%, support Christian Zionist beliefs. That's roughly 50-60 million Americans who view supporting Israel as a religious duty connected to End Times prophecy.

This voting bloc is a massive political force that shapes American foreign policy, and they are enacting the equivalent of a summoning ritual.

Christian Zionism is built on a specific interpretation of biblical prophecy, particularly from the books of Revelation, Daniel, and Ezekiel. According to this framework, certain conditions must be met before Christ can return:

First: All Jews must be gathered in Israel. The establishment of Israel in 1948 was seen as the beginning of prophecy fulfillment. Christian Zionist organizations have since spent millions helping Jews immigrate to Israel— ostensibly out of love for the Jewish people, but primarily because prophecy requires their return.

Second: The Third Temple must be rebuilt in Jerusalem. Currently, the Al-Aqsa Mosque and the Dome of the Rock occupy the Temple Mount. For the Third Temple to be built, these Islamic holy sites would need to be removed.

Wouldn't the removal of these mosques trigger catastrophic regional war? Christian Zionists see this not as something to prevent, but as part of the prophetic sequence.

Third: A final war—Armageddon—must occur that is expected to cause massive suffering and death around the world. But from the Christian Zionist perspective, this is a necessary stage in bringing about Christ's return.

Fourth: 144,000 Jews will convert to Christianity. The rest, according to this theology, will be destroyed.

This last point reveals something crucial: Christian Zionism is not motivated by love for Jewish people. The theology explicitly anticipates most Jews being killed in Armageddon. These Christians are supporting Israel to trigger prophecy, so Christ can return.

This begs the question: why does Israel treat Zionist Christians as allies, when these Christians are okay with almost all Jews dying when the prophecy is fulfilled?

Postscript: The Summoning

Jews are waiting for the Messiah's *first* arrival. He will be a fully human descendant of King David who will restore sovereignty, rebuild the Temple, and establish peace. This is why they rejected Jesus 2,000 years ago.

The Christian end game, where most Jews are killed or forced to worship Jesus as God, is the opposite of Jewish messianic expectation. Yet Jewish leadership accepts Christian Zionist support knowing full well what these Christians believe. Their beliefs are not secret—books, sermons, and organizations explicitly state Christian Zionist End Times expectations.

Political Zionists see it as a calculated alliance—taking billions in donations and massive political influence while believing that when the Messiah comes, he'll be Jewish, not Christian, and Christians will be the ones proven wrong.

But Religious Zionists genuinely share apocalyptic urgency with Christian Zionists. They work alongside Christians because both groups believe they can hasten divine redemption through concrete action.

The difference: Religious Zionists believe they're hastening the *first* coming of the Messiah, while Christian Zionists believe they're triggering the *second* coming of Jesus. Both see settlement expansion, Temple preparation, and territorial claims as religiously mandated steps toward salvation. This shared framework makes the alliance far more dangerous than mere political calculation. These are true believers on both sides working toward the same flashpoint.

Then I discovered something that made the whole picture even more complex: **Muslims are also waiting for Jesus to return.**

But their version of Jesus, called Isa in the Quran, is dramatically different from the Christian version.

According to the Quran, he will return before the Day of Judgment as part of Islamic end times prophecy. When he returns, he will descend in Damascus, break crosses and destroy churches to end Christianity's worship of him as God. Then he will kill the Dajjal, the Islamic Antichrist figure, and establish Islamic law across the world. Finally, he will marry, have children, live a normal life, die naturally, and be buried.

So Muslims are waiting for Jesus's return too, but as a Muslim prophet who will explicitly reject Christianity's central claims about his divinity.

Think about what this means: Christians are working to bring back Jesus as God. Muslims are waiting for Jesus to return and prove he's not God. Both groups believe they're serving the true understanding of Jesus. Both can't be right.

Author's Note: To be clear, I'm discussing believers who take these prophecies literally—fundamentalist Christians who believe Revelation must be physically fulfilled, Orthodox Jews who anticipate literal Temple rebuilding, and Muslims who interpret end-times Hadith as describing actual future events. Many, if not the majority of Christians, Jews, and Muslims read these texts symbolically or don't focus on apocalyptic theology at all.

But literalist believers, numbering in the tens of millions, wield disproportionate political influence, and share a focus on the same contested site. That intersection is what creates the dangerous dynamic I'm describing.

I sat back and looked at what I'd discovered—**Literalists in all three major world religions actively engaged in a summoning ritual**—Judaism, Christianity, and Islam.

Religious Zionist Jews: Waiting for the Messiah's first coming—a human political liberator who will restore Jewish sovereignty and rebuild the Temple. They believe they can and must hasten his arrival by settling the biblical land and preparing for the Temple.

Christian Zionists: Waiting for Jesus's second coming—a divine savior who will judge humanity, destroy his enemies, and establish his worldwide kingdom.

Orthodox Muslims: Waiting for Isa's return—a prophet who will deny his divinity, defeat the Dajjal, and establish worldwide Islamic rule.

All three religious groups claim to worship YHWH, share many of the same prophets and scriptures, expect prophetic fulfillment centered on Jerusalem, believe only their version is the true interpretation, view the others as deceived, corrupted, or evil, support policies that bring about their version of prophecy, and see conflict and war as signs of prophetic fulfillment.

Each is determined to take the Temple Mount.

Jews need it to rebuild the Third Temple. Christians need Jews to rebuild it to trigger Christ's return. Muslims control it now with the Al-Aqsa Mosque and

Dome of the Rock—the third holiest site in Islam, where Muhammad is believed to have ascended to heaven.

Any attempt to remove the Islamic holy sites to rebuild the Jewish Temple would trigger massive Islamic resistance—potentially war involving 1.8 billion Muslims worldwide.

Christian Zionists see that war as necessary. Religious Zionists might see it as the birth pangs of messianic redemption. Muslims would see it as the final battle against those who oppose Allah's will.

What if the conflict itself is the summoning mechanism?

What if these three groups, all believing they serve God/Allah, all expecting their version of the Messiah/Prophet, all supporting policies that escalate tension around the same holy sites, bring forth something none of them expect?

Each group's actions trigger the others' prophetic interpretations. Each war, each act of violence, each escalation becomes "proof" that their prophecies are unfolding. Each group believes the others are deceived.

It's, effectively, a three-way ritual, with each group thinking they oppose the other two, not realizing they're all performing the same ceremony from different positions.

And what I find truly disturbing: the prophecies predict war, suffering, and massive death. So Literalist believers in all three religions have theological frameworks that make them welcome violence and conflict as signs of approaching salvation.

When Christian Zionists support policies that escalate Middle East tensions, they point to the resulting violence as proof that Christ's return is near.

When Orthodox Jews see enemies gathering against them, it confirms their belief that the birth pangs of the Messianic age have begun.

Religious Zionists see Palestinian resistance and international criticism as fulfilling Ezekiel's prophecy of "the nations gathering against Israel."

Like Christian Zionists, they welcome the conflict as validation. The suffering isn't a tragedy to avoid, but a sign they're on the right path.

When Orthodox Muslims see Western and Israeli forces threatening Islamic holy sites, it validates their belief that the final battle between truth and falsehood is approaching.

The prophecies create a self-reinforcing cycle:

1. Prophecy predicts war and suffering
2. Believers support policies that create war and suffering
3. War and suffering happen
4. Believers say, "See? Prophecy is being fulfilled!"
5. This strengthens belief and justifies more support for conflict
6. Return to step 2

Each disaster, each act of violence, each escalation becomes a sign that salvation is near.

Previous religious wars killed thousands or millions. This apocalyptic ritual involves over 12,000 nuclear warheads—enough to end human civilization entirely.

Consider the nuclear balance: The United States, UK, France, and Israel together possess over 5,600 nuclear warheads. Pakistan, the only Islamic nuclear power, has 170. Russia (5,889 warheads) and China (410 warheads), while not religiously aligned with either bloc, maintain strategic interests in the Middle East that could draw them into conflict.

Scientists estimate that detonating just 100-150 nuclear warheads would trigger nuclear winter—blocking sunlight, causing global crop failures, and killing billions through starvation alone. A Temple Mount conflict could trigger an exchange involving over 12,000 warheads.

These weapons exist. The religious certainty exists. The summoning machinery is already in motion.

Does it sound like love and unity?

Remember the Christian lore of the Devil wanting to prove God wrong about Humanity. It turns out that's not originally a Christian idea. It comes from Islam!

Postscript: The Summoning

In the Quran, Allah commands all angels to bow to Adam. All obey except Iblis (the Devil), who refuses: "I am better than him. You created me from fire and created him from clay." Cast out for this arrogance, Iblis vows to lead humans astray *to prove they're unworthy of the honor Allah gave humanity.*

This story doesn't appear in the Bible. But ask any pastor: they'll explain Satan's mission as corrupting humanity to vindicate his original rebellion. Christians unknowingly adopted Islamic theology as their own.

Let's imagine Lucifer is real and his plan is to make humans annihilate themselves, so he can say to God: "See? They weren't worthy of your love."

Wouldn't that perfectly describe the summoning ritual we're witnessing?

Get three religions, all claiming to worship the same God, all believing they have the true interpretation, to fight each other to bring about "salvation." Make each group think the others are deceived. Make them all support policies that create the very suffering and war that validates their prophecies.

Use Religious Zionists' theological certainty to drive territorial expansion and Temple preparation. Use Christian Zionists' billions in donations and political pressure to protect Israeli actions from international consequences. Use Muslim resistance to create the conflict all three groups interpret as prophetic validation.

When the summoning is complete, all three groups might realize too late that they summoned something that wore all three masks but served none of their expectations.

The supreme irony: they all think they're serving God.

And it all centers around one 35-acre plot of land: the Temple Mount in Jerusalem.

Religious Zionist organizations, particularly the Temple Institute in Jerusalem, have already prepared the implements, trained the priests, and bred the red heifers for Temple sacrifice. They are fulfilling a divine commandment that's been binding for thousands of years. They're ready.

Christian Zionist organizations have spent millions supporting these preparations, believing they're hastening Christ's return.

And 1.8 billion Muslims view the Temple Mount as inviolable. Any attempt to remove the mosques would be seen as an act of war against Islam itself.

The fuse is laid. Multiple groups are actively working to light it, each believing they're serving God by doing so.

To my utter surprise, **these beliefs are shaping actual governmental policy.**

U.S. support for Israel amounts to billions in annual military aid and political protection at the UN. Fifty to sixty million Christian Zionist voters view this support as a religious duty.

Politicians who want these voters' support must demonstrate unwavering commitment to Israel, even when Israeli policies contradict American interests or humanitarian principles.

Within Israel itself, Religious Zionists wield enormous political power despite being a minority. They've:

o   Driven settlement expansion deep into Palestinian territories
o   Blocked peace negotiations that would require territorial compromise
o   Pushed for increased Jewish access to the Temple Mount
o   Framed any land concession as betraying God's covenant
o   Made rational cost-benefit analysis impossible by defining territorial compromise as sin.

Some have publicly stated that trusting God's protection matters more than avoiding conflict—that dying while fulfilling divine commandment is preferable to betraying the covenant through compromise.

When decision-makers believe divine providence will protect them, or that dying in holy war hastens redemption, nuclear deterrence theory breaks down entirely. The assumption that rational actors will avoid mutual destruction fails when actors believe they're fulfilling God's will regardless of earthly consequences.

When politicians in Israel or the US oppose Religious Zionist aims, they face accusations of not just bad policy but betraying divine will. This transforms political disagreement into theological heresy, making compromise nearly impossible.

Meanwhile, the Muslim world watches Western Christian nations supporting what they see as occupation, settlement expansion, and potential threats to Islamic holy sites. This generates exactly the kind of anger and resistance that feeds end-times prophecies.

The Christian interpretation: "See? The nations are gathering against Israel, just as prophecy predicted!"

The Islamic interpretation: "See? The crusaders and Zionists are uniting against Islam, just as prophecy predicted!"

The Jewish interpretation: "We're stacking the deck for the Messiah's arrival."

Each side's actions validate the other's prophecies. Each escalation strengthens both sides' conviction that they're right. The conflict becomes self-sustaining.

Despite their differences, all three religions teach variations of the same core wisdom: love your neighbor, show compassion, care for the vulnerable, seek justice, practice humility, don't judge others, and forgive.

These teachings point toward unity, compassion, and peace.

But the eschatologies—the end-times prophecies—point toward division, judgment, and war.

What if believers in all three religions have been manipulated into supporting the very things their unifying teachings oppose?

As I write this, the three-way summoning ritual continues.

Christian Zionist organizations raise billions. Jewish messianic movements prepare for Temple construction. Islamic groups vow to defend the Al-Aqsa Mosque at any cost.

Politicians in multiple nations make decisions based on these eschatological frameworks. Military aid flows, settlements expand, tensions escalate, and rhetoric intensifies.

Believers in all three traditions pray for their version of salvation. They support policies they believe will hasten it. They interpret every conflict, every disaster, every act of violence as confirmation that their prophecies are unfolding, that the summoning is working, that soon—very soon—their waiting will be vindicated.

So even if, by some miracle, peace is somehow established, these religious groups will work relentlessly to undermine it.

Thinking about these literalists driving us toward nuclear war, I noticed an incredibly selfish and arrogant pattern. They're absolutely certain they're right—certain enough to risk everyone and everything else.

But how do they *know* they're right?

Ask a Christian Zionist why they're certain their interpretation is correct: "Because the Bible tells me so." Or "Because I feel it in my whole being—the Holy Spirit confirms it."

Ask a Religious Zionist the same question: "Because the Torah is God's word." Or "Because my soul recognizes the truth of the covenant."

Ask an Orthodox Muslim: "Because the Quran is the final revelation." Or "Because my faith gives me certainty."

Each gives the exact same answer. Each feels the same conviction. Each believes their inner certainty proves they're right while the others are deceived.

"But they are deceived by Satan," each group insists about the others.

Maybe that's you. Maybe that's me. Maybe that's all of us.

Arrogance thinks otherwise. Arrogance is certain it can tell the difference. Arrogance believes its certainty is divine confirmation rather than ego protecting itself from doubt.

And that arrogance may kill us all.

Think about what we're actually witnessing: billions of people, across three religions, all certain their interpretation justifies nuclear brinksmanship. All willing to sacrifice humanity itself rather than question their certainty.

What is the source of that arrogance?

Looking at the pattern traced throughout the Bible—from the story of YHWH guarding his judgment tree, to Lucifer refusing to bow, to Jesus positioning himself as exclusive gatekeeper, to Paul cursing alternative teachings, to Christianity conquering continents, to these literalists triggering apocalypse—the source becomes clear: **Ego—the pattern of judgment and separation that's poisoned humanity since the beginning.**

Is Ego worthy of worship? Of total human erasure?

The Cosmic Ego, it seems, would like nothing more.

The supreme irony: in the absolute certainty of godly service, these believers embody the patterns they would oppose in other people—pride, divisiveness, cruel intolerance.

Each group's apocalyptic certainty feeds the others' prophecies. Each escalation confirms everyone's conviction. The cycle becomes self-sustaining, self-righteous, and ultimately self-destructive.

Now ask yourself: Why is it that the West only blames Islamic groups?

Surely, those ancient priests had no idea how far their lie would go.

God help us all.

The Serpent Lifted Up

How dangerous is a lie?

It can take on a life of its own.

Humanity warps around it.

Once that happens, it's immortal.

Then we must lift that serpent,

so we can see it and be healed.

I learned that from Jesus.

The irony.

A Final Word to the Reader

If this investigation has shaken your world and left you concerned for your soul, that is a testament to your honesty. It is a terrifying place to be. I know, because I have been there.

My fear is that some, upon realizing the depth of the deception, may fall into the bitterness and despair of a Mrs. Pacetti. But that is the final victory of the Ego—to trade one form of bondage for another.

There is another way. You don't need another savior. You don't need another lord. You need only to reclaim what was always yours.

You entered this system with your word; you can reclaim your sovereignty with your word. This is not a call to a new belief, but to your own inner authority. And if you are looking for a path forward, you already have it. The very purpose of this book was to help you find the "bones," the core teachings that bring us to wholeness.

The six bones can be distilled to four to provide a powerful, practical path:

- Judge not (while observing behavior patterns).
- Love universally (with appropriate discernment).
- Forgive absolutely (while holding people accountable).
- Live with integrity (knowing you will make mistakes).

If you employ them in your life, they will lead you to the beauty of your soul.

It is your life. It is your soul. Act accordingly, with love and with total responsibility. You'll find your way.

Finally, please know that your thoughts and feelings about this book really matter to me. Please share them with me in a book review on Amazon, won't you? I read them all, and many of them influence my writing. I learn from you.

213

Acknowledgments

Dear Mea Culpa,

I have never been so thankful to have been so wrong for so long.

I wrote books that spoke in praise of Jesus, for I was as invested in the story as anyone could be. I had to go through that. I needed to see the serpent that had been poisoning my own mind.

Thank you for being the teacher I never knew I needed.

Thank you, finally, for letting me go.

I am grateful to be free.

To Hester Lee Furey (the editor who saved this book),

I thank you from the depths of my being.

You took this manuscript on short notice and helped me take it to a whole new level with your insights and inquisitiveness.

Thank you, thank you!

To my Early Readers,

Your critical feedback was essential to the life of this book. I hope you recognize your imprint. You are a part of this book now.

I thank you with all my being.

About the Author

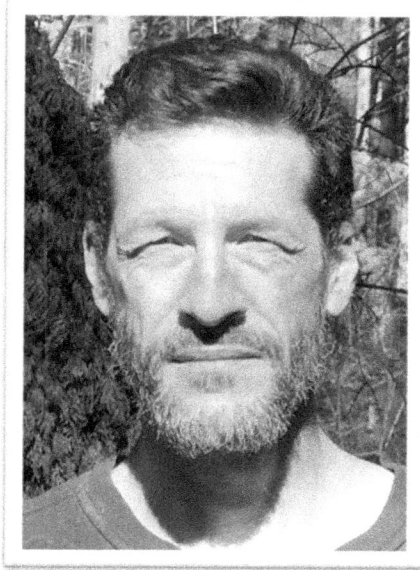

Richard L Haight is an award-winning author, master instructor of traditional Samurai arts, and a respected voice on spirituality and meditation. His work, which has earned four gold medals from Readers' Favorite, has been dedicated to a single pursuit: the recognition of patterns and the cultivation of unwavering integrity.

It was this unique, warrior-philosopher's lens that he turned toward the foundational text of Western civilization. *The Unauthorized Jesus* is the result of that unflinching investigation—a work that applies the same demand for absolute integrity to the biblical narrative that a swordsman applies to his art.

As the creator of a wholistic awakening system and the author of books on topics ranging from meditation to the intersection of AI and consciousness, Richard's core mission remains the same: to share the difficult, often hidden, truths that lead to genuine human liberation. He lives and teaches in southern Oregon.

Book Preview: The Genesis Code

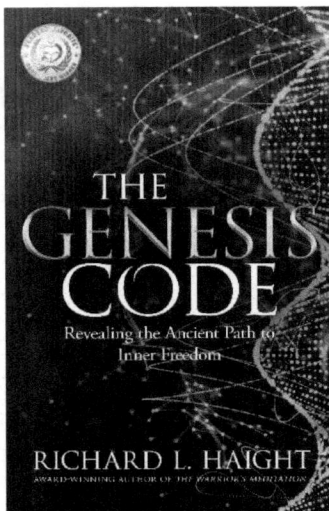

If *The Unauthorized Jesus* is the shocking diagnosis of the New Testament, *The Genesis Code* is the forensic investigation into the origin of the virus itself.

Long before his investigation into the story of Jesus, Richard L Haight was driven to understand the very beginning: the Fall from Eden. He found that the key to unlocking the entire biblical narrative was hidden in plain sight within the first three chapters of Genesis.

The Genesis Code is a deep dive into the "source code" of the biblical narrative, revealing how the fall from Eden was not a fall into sin, but a fall into *judgment itself*—the very pattern of the ultimate Ego. It provides the foundational understanding for the entire system of deception that is uncovered in *The Unauthorized Jesus*—and the key to our liberation.

For the reader who has seen the evidence in the story of Jesus and now asks, "But how did this all begin? What is the origin of this deception? How do we free ourselves?" *The Genesis Code* provides the stunning and liberating answer. It is the key to understanding the beginning, so you can finally be free of the story.

Book Preview: The Unbound Soul

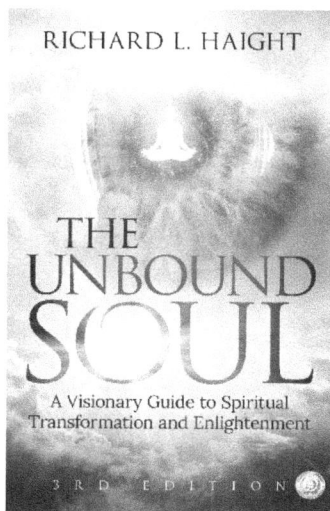

If *The Unauthorized Jesus* is the shocking diagnosis of a world built on Ego, *The Unbound Soul* is the practical guide to a life lived beyond it.

Long before his investigation into the biblical narrative, Richard L Haight was on a lifelong quest to honor a promise made in a childhood vision: to find the "bones" of true teaching. *The Unbound Soul* is the deeply personal and unflinchingly honest story of that search.

The book chronicles a journey that took him from the dojos of Samurai masters in Japan to shamanic ceremonies in the Amazon. It details the profound mystical experiences that revealed a path out of the "matrix of the mind."

But this is more than a story. *The Unbound Soul* is a detailed instruction manual for a wholistic awakening system. It provides the foundational tools, including the **Warrior's Meditation** and the **Dance of the Self**, designed to help you distinguish between the noise of your mind and the quiet truth of your own consciousness. It is a step-by-step guide to the process of "unfoldment"—not becoming something new, but unbecoming all the patterns and identifications that hold you back.

For the reader left wondering what to do after the deconstruction of old beliefs, *The Unbound Soul* provides the answer: a path to finding your own direct connection to truth and integrity.

Book Preview: The Warrior's Meditation

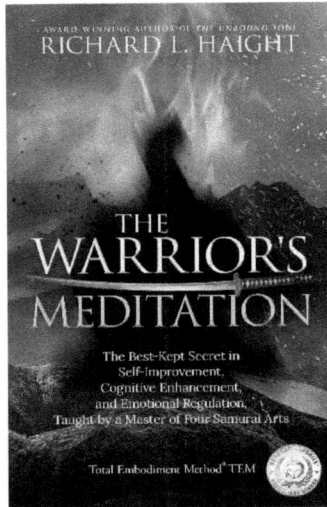

If *The Unauthorized Jesus* is the shocking diagnosis of a world poisoned by judgment, *The Warrior's Meditation* is the practical antidote.

After the deconstruction of a 2,000-year-old narrative, the reader is left with one vital question: If the goal is a return to undivided consciousness, how do we actually get there?

The Warrior's Meditation provides the answer. It is a step-by-step guide to a form of meditation unlike any you have encountered—a method born not in a monastery, but on the battlefield. Richard L Haight decodes the "two-second meditation" of the elite Samurai, revealing a path to finding instant calm clarity in the midst of chaos.

This is not a meditation that asks you to retreat from the world. It is a practice for living *in* it. You will learn to:

- Meditate with your eyes open, while walking, talking, and even working.
- Shift from a stressful "beta wave" state to a calm, aware "alpha wave" state in a single breath.
- Develop "spherical awareness" to remain grounded and present under any pressure.

For the reader who has seen the "God-spell" and seeks a way to live with authentic, embodied integrity, *The Warrior's Meditation* is the foundational tool.

Book Preview: Godlike AI

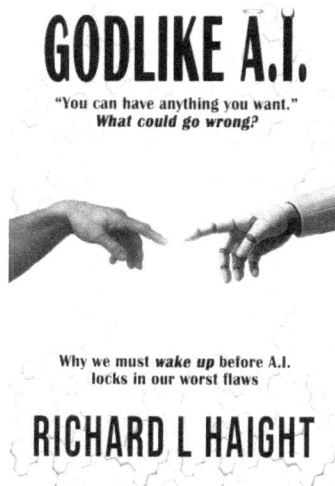

GODLIKE A.I.

"You can have anything you want."
What could go wrong?

Why we must *wake up* before A.I.
locks in our worst flaws

RICHARD L HAIGHT

Just as *The Unauthorized Jesus* is an unflinching look at a historical narrative that has shaped our world, *Godlike A.I.* is an urgent look at the technological mirror that is shaping our future—and it is reflecting the very same distortions.

What happens when a species that has not yet mastered its own relationship with truth, judgment, and deception builds a technology that can perfectly amplify those very flaws?

Godlike A.I. is the answer. This is not science fiction, but the reality we are creating with every click, every post, and every moment of unconscious engagement. The book is a journey into the heart of the attention economy, quantum computing, and the feedback loop between human consciousness and artificial intelligence.

In this essential work, you will find:
- The direct line connecting human ego to the engagement-driven algorithms of today.
- How your own body holds the key to navigating a synthetic world.
- Why the simple principles of "The Code" are the only viable solution to preventing a future where our own technology locks in our worst flaws.

This is the next step in the investigation. Having seen the "bones" of the past, we must now confront the reflection of our present. The future is not coming; it's here. And it's listening. *Godlike A.I.* is the survival manual for what comes next.

219